STUDY GUIDE
to accompany

MANAGERIAL ACCOUNTING

JAMES JIAMBALVO Ph.D., C.P.A.
PricewaterhouseCoopers and Alumni Endowed Professor of Accounting
University of Washington— Seattle
Seattle, Washington

Authored by
JESSICA JOHNSON FRAZIER D.B.A.
Associate Professor of Accounting
Eastern Kentucky University

PATRICIA MOUNCE Ph.D., C.P.A
Associate Professor of Accounting
Mississippi College

John Wiley & Sons, Inc.
New York • Chichester • Weinheim • Brisbane • Singapore • Toronto

To order books or for customer service call 1-800-CALL-WILEY (225-5945).

ISBN 0-471-28349-5

Printed in the United States of America

10 9 8 7 6 5 4 3 2 1

Printed and bound by Bradford & Bigelow, Inc.

Contents

Chapter 1   Introduction to Managerial Accounting 1

Chapter 2   Manufacturing Costs and Job-Order Costing Systems 18

Chapter 3   Process Costing 43

Chapter 4   Cost-Volume-Profit Analysis 64

Chapter 5   Cost Allocation and Activity-Based Costing 86

Chapter 6   The Use of Cost Information in Management Decision Making 106

Chapter 7   Capital Budgeting Decisions 123

Chapter 8   Budgetary Planning and Control 138

Chapter 9   Standard Costs and Variance analysis 161

Chapter 10   Decentralization and Performance Evaluation 179

CHAPTER 1

INTRODUCTION TO MANAGERIAL ACCOUNTING

CHAPTER INTRODUCTION

Financial accounting stresses accounting concepts and procedures that relate to preparing reports for external users of accounting information. In comparison, **managerial accounting** stresses accounting concepts and procedures that are relevant to preparing reports for internal users of accounting information. This chapter provides an overview of the role of managerial accounting in planning, control, and decision making. It also defines important cost concepts, introduces key ideas that will be used throughout the text, and discusses the role of the controller as the top management accountant.

Objectives, Terms, and Discussions

LO1 *State the primary goal of managerial accounting.*

Managers need to plan and control their operations and make a variety of decisions. The goal of managerial accounting is to provide the information managers need for planning, control, and decision making.

LO2 *Describe how budgets are used in planning.*

A plan communicates a company's goals to employees and specifies the resources needed to achieve them. The financial plans prepared by managerial accountants are referred to as **budgets**. For example, a profit budget indicates planned income, a cash-flow budget indicates planned cash inflows and outflows, and a production budget indicates the planned quantity of production and the expected cost.

LO3   *Describe how performance reports are used in the control process.*

Control of organizations is achieved by evaluating the performance of managers and the operations for which they are responsible. Managers are evaluated to ascertain how their performances should be rewarded or punished, motivating them to perform at a high level. Evaluations of managers are typically tied to compensation and promotion opportunities. Operations are evaluated to provide information as to whether or not they should be changed. An evaluation of an operation can be negative even when the evaluation of the manager responsible for the operation is basically positive.

Company plans often play an important role in the control process. Managers can compare actual results with planned results and decide if corrective action is needed. Actual results may differ from the plan for several reasons.
- The plan may not have been followed properly.
- The plan may not have been well thought out.
- Changing circumstances may have made the plan out of date.

The reports used to evaluate the performance of managers and the operations they control are referred to as **performance reports**. Typically, performance reports only suggest areas that should be investigated; they do not provide definitive information on performance. A performance report frequently involves a comparison of current period performance with prior period performance or with planned (budgeted) performance. Managers use performance reports to "flag" areas that need closer attention and to avoid areas that appear to be under control. For example, a manager would not investigate rent if the actual costs were equal to the planned level of costs. Managers typically follow the principle of **management by exception** when using performance reports. This means that managers investigate departures from the plan that appear to be exceptional; they do not investigate minor departures from the plan.

Decision making is an integral part of the planning and control process; decisions are made to reward or punish managers, to change operations, or to revise plans. Chapter 6 is devoted to the topic of decision making. One of the two key ideas discussed later in this chapter relates to decision making and its focus on so-called incremental analysis.

LO4   *Distinguish between financial and managerial accounting.*

There are several important differences between managerial and financial accounting.

1. Managerial accounting is directed at internal rather than external users of accounting information. External users include investors, creditors, and government agencies that use information to make investment, lending, and regulation decisions. Internal managers need information for planning, control, and decision making.

2. Managerial accounting may deviate from generally accepted accounting principles (GAAP). Companies prepare financial accounting information in accordance with GAAP to satisfy creditors, investors, and governmental agencies. Managerial accounting is completely optional and stresses information that is useful to internal managers for planning, control, and decision making. If deviating from GAAP will provide more useful information to internal managers, GAAP need not be followed.

3. Managerial accounting may present more detailed information. Financial accounting presents information in a highly summarized form. For example, net income is presented for the company as a whole. Managers need more detailed information. For example, information about the cost of

operating individual departments is needed by internal managers in addition to the cost of operating the company as a whole.

4. Managerial accounting may present more nonmonetary information. Both managerial and financial accounting reports generally contain monetary information. However, managerial accounting reports also contain a substantial amount of nonmonetary information. For example, the quantity of material consumed in production, the number of hours worked by employees, and the number of product defects are important data that appear in managerial accounting reports.

5. Managerial accounting places more emphasis on the future. Financial accounting is concerned with presenting the results of past transactions. One of the primary purposes of managerial accounting is planning which involves estimating the costs and benefits of future transactions.

Several differences between managerial and financial accounting have been presented. However, external and internal users often seek similar information. Managers make significant use of financial accounting reports, and external users occasionally request financial information that is appropriate for internal users. For example, creditors may request a detailed cash-flow projection.

LO5   *Define cost terms used in planning, control, and decision making.*

Variable costs are costs that increase or decrease in response to increases or decreases in the level of business activity. Examples of variable costs are direct material and direct labor. Variable cost per unit does not change when production changes. For example, suppose XYZ Company incurred $15,000 of variable material cost in the prior month when production was 5,000 units. How much variable cost should be incurred in the current month if production is expected to increase by 20 percent to 6,000 units? If production increases by 20 percent, the variable cost would be expected to increase to $18,000 ($15,000 × 120%). Note that the variable cost per unit remains $3 per unit ($18,000/6,000 units).

    Fixed costs are costs that do not change with changes in the level of business activity. Examples of fixed costs are administrative salaries and rent. Suppose that in the prior month, XYZ Company incurred $10,000 of rent. If the company increases production from 5,000 to 6,000 units, the level of rent should remain the same. The cost per unit of fixed costs does change when there are changes in production. When production increases, the constant amount of fixed cost is spread over a larger number of units. This drives down the fixed cost per unit. At an activity level of 5,000 units, the fixed cost per unit is $2 ($10,000/5,000) but at an activity level of 6,000 units, the fixed cost per unit is driven down to $1.67 ($10,000/6,000).

    Costs incurred in the past are referred to as **sunk costs**. Sunk costs are not relevant to present decisions, because they do not change when these decisions are made. Assume that after you purchase a ticket to a concert for $20, your father invites you to a professional football game scheduled for the same night. The cost of the concert ticket is irrelevant to the decision as to whether or not you should go to the ball game. What is relevant is how much you will enjoy the ball game versus the concert and the amount for which you can sell the concert ticket. The $20 price of the ticket is a sunk cost.

    Opportunity costs are the values of benefits foregone when one decision alternative is selected over another. For example, XYZ Company declines an order to produce 800 units for a competitor of its largest regular customer because taking the order will jeopardize the company's relationship with its regular customer. If the order would have generated $2,000 additional revenue and $1,500 additional costs, the opportunity cost is $500 (the net benefit foregone).

    Direct costs are cost that are directly traced to a product, activity, or department. **Indirect costs** are those that either cannot be directly traced to a product, activity, or department, or are not worth tracing.

A manager can influence a **controllable cost**, but cannot influence a **noncontrollable cost**. A distinction between controllable and noncontrollable costs is especially important when evaluating manager performance. A manager should not be evaluated unfavorably if a noncontrollable cost sharply increases.

LO6   *Explain the two key ideas in managerial accounting.*

Decision making relies on incremental analysis. Essentially, **incremental analysis** involves the calculation of the difference in revenue and the difference in cost between decision alternatives. The difference in revenue is the incremental revenue of one alternative over another, whereas the difference in cost is the incremental cost of one alternative over another. If an alternative yields an incremental profit, it is the preferred alternative.

You get what you measure. In other words, performance measures greatly influence the behavior of managers. Companies can select from a vast number of performance measures. Examples of performance measures include profit, market share, sales to new customers, product development time, number of defective units, and number of late deliveries.

LO7   *Discuss the duties of the controller, the treasurer, and the chief financial officer (CFO.)*

The **controller** prepares reports for planning and evaluating company activities (e.g., budgets and performance reports) and provides the information needed to make management decisions (e.g., decisions related to adding or dropping a product). The controller may also be responsible for filing all financial accounting reports and tax returns with the Internal Revenue Service and other taxing agencies, as well as coordinating the activities with the firm's external auditors. Most companies want controllers who have the capacity to be an integral part of the top management team. Not only does the controller need strong accounting skills, but also excellent written and oral communication skills, solid interpersonal skills, and a deep knowledge of the industry in which the firm competes.

The **treasurer** has custody of cash and funds invested in various marketable securities. In addition to money management duties, the treasurer is generally responsible for maintaining relationships with investors, banks, and other creditors. The treasurer plays a major role in managing cash and marketable securities, preparing cash forecasts, and obtaining financing from banks and other lenders. Both the controller and the treasurer report to the **chief financial officer (CFO)** who is the senior executive responsible for both accounting and financial operations.

Review of Key Terms

Budget: A formal document that quantifies a company's plan for achieving its goals.

Chief financial officer (CFO): The senior executive responsible for accounting and financial operations.

Controllable cost: A cost that a manager can influence by the decisions he or she makes.

Controller: The top accounting executive responsible for financial and managerial accounting information and tax filings.

Direct cost: A cost that is directly traceable to a product, activity, or department.

Fixed cost: Costs that do not change when there is a change in business activity.

Incremental analysis: An analysis of the revenues and costs that will change if a decision alternative is selected.

Indirect cost: A cost that either is not directly traceable to a product, activity, or department or is not worth tracing.

Management by exception: Policy by which managers investigate departures from planned results that appear to be exceptional; they do not investigate minor departures from the plan.

Managerial accounting: Accounting that stresses concepts and procedures relevant to preparing reports for internal users of accounting information. It focuses on information that is useful in planning, control, and decision making.

Noncontrollable cost: A cost that managers cannot influence.

Opportunity cost: The values of benefits foregone by selecting one decision alternative over another.

Performance report: Report used to evaluate managers and the operations they control. Frequently, performance reports involve a comparison of planned and actual results.

Sunk cost: Cost incurred in the past—they are irrelevant to current decisions.

Treasurer: Company official who has custody of cash and funds invested in various marketable securities. In addition to money management duties, the treasurer is generally responsible for maintaining relationships with investors, banks, and other creditors.

Variable cost: Those costs that increase or decrease in response to increases or decreases in business activity.

Chapter 1 – True/False

___F___ 1. Managerial accounting stresses accounting concepts and procedures that are relevant to preparing reports for external users of financial information.

___F___ 2. A negative evaluation of an operation will always result in a negative evaluation of the manager responsible for the operation.

___T___ 3. Performance reports frequently involve a comparison of current period performance with performance of a prior period or with planned performance.

___F___ 4. Most managers do not need to plan and control their operations.

___T___ 5. A production budget indicates the planned quantity of production and the expected cost.

___T___ 6. One difference between managerial accounting and financial accounting is that managerial accounting may deviate from GAAP.

___F___ 7. Sunk costs are relevant to present decisions.

___T___ 8. Both the controller and the treasurer report to the chief financial officer.

___T___ 9. Decision making relies on incremental analysis.

___T___ 10. Performance measures greatly influence the behavior of managers.

___F___ 11. The controller has custody of cash and funds invested in various marketable securities

___T___ 12. A plan communicates a company's goals to employees and specifies the resources needed to achieve them.

Chapter 1 – Key Terms Matching

Match the terms found in Chapter 1 with the following definitions:

a. budgets
b. controllable cost
c. controller
d. direct cost
e. fixed cost
f. incremental analysis

g. indirect cost
h. noncontrollable cost
i. opportunity cost
j. performance report
k. sunk cost
l. variable cost

___K___   1. Costs incurred in the past that are not relevant to present decisions

___I___   2. The benefits foregone when one decision alternative is selected over another

___E___   3. Costs that do not change with changes in the level of business activity

___G___   4. Costs that either cannot be directly traced to a product, activity, or department

___B___   5. Costs which a manager can control

___J___   6. Reports used to evaluate performance of managers and the operations they control

___A___   7. The financial plans prepared by a managerial accountant

___F___   8. The calculation of the difference in revenue and the difference in cost between decision alternatives

___L___   9. Costs that increase or decrease in response to increases or decreases in the level of business activity

___C___ 10. The top managerial accounting position

___D___ 11. Costs that are directly traceable to a product, activity, or department

___h___ 12. Costs which a manager cannot control

Chapter 1 – Multiple Choice

1.   When following the principle of management by exception, managers
   a.   investigate departures from the plan that appear to be exceptional.
   b.   do not investigate minor departures from the plan.
   c.   both a and b above.
   d.   none of the above.

2.   Performance reports
    a.   must be prepared in a generally accepted method.
    b.   are used to compare current period performance with prior period performance.
    c.   are used to compare current period performance with budgeted performance.
    d.   both b and c above.

3.   Compared to financial accounting, managerial accounting places more emphasis on
    a.   information for external users.
    b.   the future.
    c.   generally accepted accounting principles (GAAP).
    d.   information in a highly summarized form.

4.   With respect to a variable cost
    a.   the per unit cost is constant.
    b.   the total cost varies in direct proportion with the level of activity.
    c.   the per unit varies inversely with the level of activity.
    d.   both a and b above.

5.   With respect to a fixed cost
    a.   the per unit cost varies inversely with the level of activity.
    b.   the total is constant.
    c.   the total cost varies in direct proportion with the level of activity.
    d.   both a and b above.

6.   Which of the following would be considered a variable cost?
    a.   Rent
    b.   Depreciation
    c.   Property taxes
    d.   Fruit filling used in the production of Marie's pies

7.   Which of the following is **not** a management function?
    a.   Planning
    b.   Directing
    c.   Chastising
    d.   Controlling

8.   Sunk costs are
    a.   costs that were incurred in the past.
    b.   not relevant to present decisions.
    c.   do not change.
    d.   all of the above.

9.   Opportunity costs are
    a.   the values of benefits foregone when one decision alternative is selected over another.
    b.   not relevant in a decision making scenario.
    c.   both a and b above.
    d.   none of the above.

10   Direct costs are costs that are
    a.   not relevant in a decision making scenario.
    b.   cannot be directly traced to a product, activity of department.
    c.   traceable to a product, activity of department.
    d.   both a and c above.

11.   The Institute of Management Accounting (IMA) is a professional organization that
    a.   publishes the monthly magazine *Strategic Finance.*
    b.   conducts a comprehensive examination to test the knowledge of management account-ants wanting to achieve the designation of Certified Management Accountant (CMA).
    c.   develops standards of ethical conduct for Management Accountants.
    d.   all of the above.

12.   The top managerial accounting position is held by the
    a.   bean counter.
    b.   treasurer.
    c.   chief financial officer.
    d.   controller.

Exercise 1 – 1 The goal of managerial accounting is to provide information managers need for (1) planning, (2) controlling and (3) decision making.

    1.   Describe each of the three managerial responsibilities.

    2.   Give examples of each of the three managerial responsibilities.

Exercise 1 – 2   Assume you have just started an intern position in the Human Resources Department at Vicious Cycle Bike, Inc. You have had one course in accounting, Introduction to Financial Accounting.   However, you know very little about managerial accounting. The controller called and asked you to place an ad in the local newspaper for a managerial accountant. Write an ad to appear in the *Gwinnet Gazette.*

Exercise 1 – 3   Assume your roommate just walked in from class and announced, "I don't need to take managerial accounting. I am a management major." Based on the information in the first chapter of your managerial accounting text and other information you may find in the library, write a response to your roommate.

Problem 1 – 4 Assume that you are the controller of Vicious Cycle, Inc., a large manufacturer of racing bikes. The following information is available for the two most recent years:

	2005	2004
Number of bikes produced	100,000	90,000
Direct materials	$4,000,000	$3,600,000
Direct labor	6,000,000	5,400,000
Rent	500,000	500,000
Insurance	20,000	20,000
Supervisory salaries	15,000	15,000
Total budgeted production cost	$10,535,000	$9,355,000

1.   Identify the behavior of each following expenses as variable or fixed cost.

   a.   Direct materials _____

   b.   Direct labor _____

   c.   Rent _____

   d.   Insurance _____

   e.   Supervisory salaries_____

2.   Assume Mr. Pedal, president of Vicious Cycle, has told you that in the year 2006, the company expects to manufacture and sell 125,000 bikes. Prepare a budget of production costs for Vicious Cycle at this level of sales.

_____

_____

_____

_____

_____

_____

_____

_____

Problem 1 – 5 Assume that in 2006, Vicious Cycle actually produced and sold 125,500 bicycles and incurred the following costs:

Number of bikes produced	125,500
Direct materials	$5,020,000
Direct labor	7,530,000
Rent	500,000
Insurance	20,000
Supervisory salaries	15,000
Total production cost	$13,085,000

1. Prepare a performance report for production costs for the year 2006

_____

_____

_____

_____

_____

_____

_____

_____

_____

2. Mr. Pedal is concerned because in some instances actual costs exceeded budgeted costs. Are his concerns justified? Why or why not?

_____

_____

3. Mr. Pedal has noticed that the cost per bike has decreased with the level of production shown in Problems 1-4 and 1-5 (90,000, 100,000, and 125,000). Compute the cost per bike and explain to Mr. Pedal why the cost per bike is different in each case.

_____

_____

_____

Solutions – True/False

1.	F	Managerial accounting stresses accounting concepts and procedures that are relevant to preparing reports for internal users of financial information.
2.	F	A negative evaluation of an operation does not always result in a negative evaluation of the manager responsible for the operation.
3.	T	
4.	F	Managers do need to plan and control their operations
5.	T	
6.	T	
7.	F	Sunk costs are not relevant to present decisions.
8.	T	
9.	T	
10.	T	
11.	F	The treasurer has custody of cash and funds invested in various marketable securities
12.	T	

Solutions – Key Terms Matching

1.	k. sunk cost		7.	a. budget
2.	i. opportunity cost		8.	f. incremental analysis
3.	e. fixed cost		9.	l. variable cost
4.	g. indirect cost		10.	c. controller
5.	b. controllable cost		11.	d. direct cost
6.	j. performance report		12.	h. noncontrollable cost

Solutions – Multiple Choice

1.	c		7.	c
2.	d		8.	d
3.	b		9.	a
4.	d		10.	c
5.	d		11.	d
6.	d		12.	d

Solution – Exercise 1 – 1
The goal of managerial accounting is to provide information managers need for (1) planning, (2) controlling and (3) decision making.

1. Describe each of the three managerial responsibilities.

    a. **Planning** is a key activity for managers. Plans may be long range such as deciding what type business to go into, where the business should be located, or what niche the business will fill. Other plans may be intermediate in range. For example, planning to buy a new piece of equipment would be intermediate in terms of time period. When directing and motivating employees on a daily basis, managers make short range plans.

    b. **Control** of organizations is achieved by evaluating the performance of managers and the operations for which they are responsible. In the control phase, the actual results are compared with the budgeted results to see if the plans of the company are being carried out.

    c. **Decision Making** is an integral part of the planning and control process. When planning and controlling, managers are constantly making decisions.

2. Give examples of each of the three managerial responsibilities.

    a. **Planning** – what type business to enter; where the business is to be located; what niche the business will fill; what type furniture and equipment will be needed

    b. **Control** – compare actual achievements to budgeted amounts. The comparison can be with sales in units, dollar amounts, or expense items – both variable and fixed

    c. **Decision Making** – When planning or controlling, decision making is an ongoing process. Managers must constantly make decisions. The decisions may focus on how many employees are needed, who to hire, how to price merchandise, what hours the business will be open, etc.

Solution – Exercise 1 – 2
Assume you have just started an intern position in the Human Resources Department at Vicious Cycle Bike, Inc. You have had one course in accounting, Introduction to Financial Accounting. However, you know very little about managerial accounting. The controller called and asked you to place an ad in the local newspaper for a managerial accountant. Write an ad to appear in the *Gwinnet Gazette*.

> We are a large, rapidly growing business specializing in custom designed performance bikes. We currently have an opening for a Managerial Accountant to direct financial activities, including the preparation of financial budgets, forecasts and analysis. The ideal candidate will have a four-year degree in accounting, demonstrate strong communication skills, and be able to make decisions. Candidate should have 5 years experience. A CMA is a plus. Excellent opportunity and salary.

Solution – Exercise 1 – 3 Assume your roommate just walked in from class and announced, "I don't need to take managerial accounting. I am a management major." Based on the information in the first chapter of your managerial accounting text and other information you may find in the library, write a response to your roommate.

Dear Roomie,

　　Management accounting is a challenging course. I can understand your frustrations. However, you will find it difficult to succeed as a manager without management accounting as a tool. As you learned in the first chapter of your management accounting text, "the primary goal of managerial accounting is to provide information that helps managers plan and control company activities and make business decisions." Management accounting produces information concerning the economic condition of the enterprise, such as the cost and profitability of the organization's products, services, and activities. Management accounting also provides information on the economic performance of decentralized operating units, such as business units, divisions and departments. A good understanding of management accounting will make you a better manager.

Your roommate

Solution – Problem 1 – 4

Assume that you are the controller of Vicious Cycle, Inc., a large manufacturer of racing bikes. The following information is available for the two most recent years:

	2005	2004
Number of bikes produced	100,000	90,000
Direct materials	$4,000,000	$3,600,000
Direct labor	6,000,000	5,400,000
Rent	500,000	500,000
Insurance	20,000	20,000
Supervisory salaries	15,000	15,000
Total budgeted production cost	$14,465,000	$12,965,000

1. Identify the behavior of each following expenses as variable or fixed cost.

   a. Direct materials – Variable cost
   b. Direct labor – Variable cost
   c. Rent – Fixed cost
   d. Insurance – Fixed cost
   e. Supervisory salaries – Fixed cost

2. Assume Mr. Pedal, president of Vicious Cycle, has told you that in the year 2006, the company expects to manufacture and sell 125,000 bikes. Prepare a budget of production costs for Vicious Cycle at this level of sales.

Direct materials (125,000 @ $40)	$5,000,000
Direct Labor (125,000 @ $60)	7,500,000
Rent	500,000
Insurance	20,000
Supervisory salaries	15,000
Total budgeted production cost	$13,035,000

Solution – Problem 1 – 5 Assume that in 2006 Vicious Cycle actually produced and sold 125,500 bicycles and incurred the following cost:

Number of bikes produced	125,500
Direct materials	$5,020,000
Direct labor	7,530,000
Rent	500,000
Insurance	20,000
Supervisory salaries	15,000
Total production cost	$13,085,000

1. Prepare a performance report for the year 2006

	Budget 125,000	Actual 125,500	Budgeted Minus Actual
Direct materials	$ 5,000,000	$ 5,020,000	($20,000)
Direct Labor	7,500,000	7,530,000	(30,000)
Rent	500,000	500,000	-0-
Insurance	20,000	20,000	-0-
Supervisory salaries	15,000	15,000	-0-
Total production cost	$13,035,000	$13,085,000	($50,000)

2. Mr. Pedal is concerned because in some instances actual costs exceeded budgeted costs? Are his concerns justified? Why or why not?

> No, Mr. Pedal's concerns are not justified. Vicious cycle budgeted to manufacture and sell 125,000 bikes. However, the company actually manufactured and sold 125,500 bikes. It is reasonable that it would cost more to make 125,500 bikes than it would cost to make 125,000 bikes.

3. Mr. Pedal has noticed that the cost per bike has decreased with the level of production shown in Problems 1-4 and 1-5 (90,000, 100,000, and 125,000). Compute the cost per bike and explain to Mr. Pedal why the cost per bike is different in each case.

> $ 9,535,000/ 90,000 bikes = $105.94
> $10,535,000/100,000 bikes = $105.35
> $13,035,000/125,000 bikes = $104.28
> $13,085,000/125,500 bikes = $104.26

If all of the expenses were variable expenses unit cost would be the constant at each level of activity. However, when both fixed and variable costs are present, the greater the level of production the lower the cost per unit. At a greater level of production, fixed costs are being spread over a greater number of units.

CHAPTER **2**

MANUFACTURING COSTS AND JOB-ORDER COSTING SYSTEMS

CHAPTER INTRODUCTION

Manufacturing costs include material, labor, and overhead. A **product costing system** is used to measure and record the cost of manufactured products. This chapter introduces cost terms and shows how the costs are reflected in the financial statements. Two types of costing systems are presented and a job-order costing system is demonstrated for both manufacturing and service organizations. Changes in manufacturing practices and how these changes are helping companies succeed in a competitive global economy are also discussed.

Objectives, Terms, and Discussions

LO1 *Distinguish between manufacturing and nonmanufacturing costs and between product and period costs.*

A company needs to know the cost of its products for several reasons:
- to set prices
- to calculate profit when products are sold
- to prepare financial statements in accordance with generally accepted accounting principles (GAAP)
- to assess the reasonableness of the cost incurred in purchasing or manufacturing products
- for management decision-making

The cost of a merchandising firm's product is relatively simple to calculate: the cost includes the purchase price (net of returns, allowances, and discounts) plus shipping costs. Calculating the cost of a manufacturing firm's product is more complex. It includes the costs of raw materials used plus labor costs and any other manufacturing costs incurred in the manufacturing process.

Costs are classified as manufacturing and nonmanufacturing costs and also as product and period costs. Product costs are considered an asset (inventory) until the finished goods are sold and become an expense (cost of goods sold). This ensures a proper matching of revenue with the costs necessary to produce the revenue.

Manufacturing costs are all the costs associated with the production of goods. They include three cost categories: direct material, direct labor, and manufacturing overhead. **Direct material cost** is the cost of all materials and parts that are directly traced to items produced. Examples of direct materials are the wood, steering assembly, and motor used to make a boat. **Indirect material cost** is the cost of all materials and parts that are not directly traced to a product. Examples of indirect materials are the glue and screws used to make a boat. **Direct labor cost** is the cost of labor that is directly traced to items produced. An example of a direct labor cost is the cost of the workers directly involved in constructing a boat. **Indirect labor cost** is the cost of labor that is not traced directly to items produced. An example of an indirect labor cost is the cost of a production supervisor. **Manufacturing overhead** is the cost of all manufacturing activities other than direct material and direct labor. It includes indirect material, indirect labor, and a wide variety of other cost items. Examples of manufacturing overhead include the cost of indirect material, indirect labor, glue, supervisory salaries, depreciation of tools, utilities, and a number of other items.

Nonmanufacturing costs are all the costs that are not associated with the production of goods. Examples of nonmanufacturing costs include selling and general and administrative costs. **Selling costs** include all the costs associated with securing and filling customer orders. Examples of selling costs include advertising costs and sales personnel salaries. **General and administrative costs** are all the costs associated with the firm's general management. Examples of general and administrative costs include salaries of the company president and general managers and the costs of supplies used by clerical employees.

Product costs (also called *manufacturing costs*) are those costs assigned to goods produced. Product costs include direct material, direct labor, and manufacturing overhead. **Period costs** (*nonmanufacturing costs*) are identified with accounting periods rather than with goods produced. Examples of period costs are selling and general and administrative costs.

Full cost means that product cost information used to prepare financial statements includes both variable and fixed manufacturing overhead as well as direct material and direct labor, which are generally variable costs. GAAP requires that inventory and cost of goods sold be presented using full cost information.

LO2   *Discuss the three inventory accounts of a manufacturing firm.*

Product costs are treated as an asset until the finished goods are sold. Product costs appear on the balance sheet in three asset accounts related to inventory: Raw Materials, Work in Process, and Finished Goods. The **Raw Materials Inventory** account includes the cost of materials on hand that are used to produce a company's products. Examples of Raw Material Inventory include steering assemblies, wood, motors, screws, and glue used to make a boat. **Work in Process Inventory** is the inventory account for the cost of goods that are only partially completed. For example, if a boat is partially completed at the end of a period, the cost of direct material, direct labor, and manufacturing overhead incurred to bring the boat into its current state of partial completion is included in Work in Process Inventory. **Finished Goods Inventory** is the account for the cost of all items that are complete and ready to sell. Finished Goods Inventory includes the cost of direct material, direct labor, and manufacturing overhead incurred to bring those boats to their finished state.

LO3   *Describe the flow of product costs in a manufacturing firm's accounts.*

In an accounting system, product costs flow from one inventory account to another. The cost of direct material used reduces the Raw Material Inventory account and increases the Work in Process Inventory account. The cost of indirect material used reduces the Raw Material Inventory account and increases the Manufacturing Overhead account. The amount of direct labor increases the Work in Process account, but indirect labor is accumulated in the Manufacturing Overhead account. The Manufacturing Overhead account is then periodically added to the Work in Process account. Once items are finished, the cost of the completed items is transferred from the Work in Process account to the Finished Goods account.

The **cost of goods manufactured** refers to the cost of all goods completed during the period. When the completed items are sold, the cost of the items sold is considered an expense and must be transferred from Finished Goods into Cost of Goods Sold. This matches revenue (sales dollars) with the cost of producing the revenue (cost of goods sold). Illustration 2-6 in the textbook presents a Schedule of Cost of Goods Manufactured and the related Income Statement.

In a manufacturing entity, before cost of goods sold can be calculated, the cost of goods manufactured must be calculated. Cost of goods manufactured is calculated by adding to the beginning balance in Work in Process the current manufacturing cost (direct material, direct labor, and manufacturing overhead incurred in the current period) and deducting the ending balance in Work in Process.

Beginning Balance in Work In Process	+	Current Manufacturing Costs	-	Ending Balance in Work in Process	=	Costs of Goods Manufactured

The cost of goods available for sale is the sum of the beginning balance in Finished Goods Inventory plus cost of goods manufactured. Cost of goods sold is then calculated by adding to the beginning balance in Finished Goods Inventory the cost of goods manufactured and deducting the ending balance in Finished Goods Inventory.

Beginning Balance in Finished Goods	+	Cost of Goods Manufactured	-	Ending Balance in Finished Goods	=	Cost of Goods Sold

LO4   *Discuss the types of product costing systems.*

There are two major product costing systems: job-order costing systems and process costing systems. Companies that produce individual products or batches of products that are unique use a **job-order costing system**. Examples of companies using job-order systems include construction companies, printing companies, or consulting companies. A **job** is an individual product or batch for which a company needs cost information. When the items that make up the job are completed and sold, the company can match the cost of the job with the revenue it produces and attain an appropriate measure of profit.

Companies that generally produce large quantities of identical items use **a process costing system**. Examples of companies using process costing systems include metal producers, chemical producers, and producers of paints and plastics. These products pass through uniform and continuous production operations. As one can see in Chapter 3, costs are accumulated by each operation, and the unit cost of items is determined by dividing the costs of the production operations by the number of identical items produced.

$$\text{Unit cost of items produced} = \frac{\text{Total cost of production}}{\text{Total number of units produced}}$$

In a job-order costing system, costs are traced to specific jobs or items produced. However, in a process costing system, there is no need to trace costs to specific jobs or items produced since all the items are virtually identical.

LO5 *Explain the relation between the cost of jobs and the Work in Process Inventory, Finished Goods Inventory, and Cost of Goods Sold accounts.*

Product costs include three cost items: direct material, direct labor, and manufacturing overhead. In a job-order costing system, the cost of a job is the total of these three items. Consequently, when using a job-order system you must relate these costs to specific jobs.

Product costs are reflected in one of three accounts: Work in Process Inventory (includes the cost of jobs that are currently being worked on) or Finished Goods Inventory (includes the cost of jobs complete but not sold) on the balance sheet or in Cost of Goods Sold (includes the cost of jobs that are sold during the accounting period) on the income statement. The flow of costs through a job-order costing system is based on the status of jobs. First, direct material, direct labor, and manufacturing overhead costs related to jobs being worked on are added to the Work in Process Inventory account. Then, as specific jobs are completed, the costs of those jobs are deducted from Work in Process Inventory and added to the Finished Goods Inventory account. Finally, as specific jobs are sold, the costs of those jobs are deducted from Finished Goods Inventory and added to Cost of Goods Sold.

Remember the two components of a job-costing system:
- The items making up the costs of a job (direct material, direct labor, and overhead)
- The way the status of jobs triggers the flow of costs through financial statement accounts (Work in Process, Finished Goods, and Cost of Goods Sold)

LO6 *Describe how direct material, direct labor, and manufacturing overhead are assigned to jobs.*

Job-order costing operations begin when a company decides to produce a specific product for stock or accepts an order for a custom product. When a company accepts an order, a job-cost sheet is prepared. A **job-cost sheet** is a form used to accumulate the costs of producing the item or items ordered. The job-cost sheet contains detailed information on the three categories of product costs: direct material, direct labor, and manufacturing overhead.

A **material requisition form** is used to request the release of materials from a company's storage area. The form lists the materials required and the number of the job requiring the materials. Each material requisition form is listed in summary form on the job cost sheet. Removal of materials from storage for use on specific job decreases the Raw Materials Inventory account and increases the Work in Process Inventory account. The entry to record the removal of materials from storage for use in a specific job is:

Work in Process Inventory	XXX	
Raw Materials Inventory		XXX

Time tickets (also called job tickets or work tickets) are filled out by workers in a company that uses a job-order costing system. Time tickets are used to keep track of the amount of time spent on each job. Periodically, the amount of direct labor cost attributed to jobs being worked on must be debited to the Work in Process account. The appropriate journal entry is:

Work in Process Inventory	XXX	
Wages Payable		XXX

The final cost component to assign to a job is manufacturing overhead. Manufacturing overhead costs are indirectly traced to goods produced and, therefore, must be allocated to jobs. The basic approach involves spreading the overhead among the various jobs based on some characteristic that jobs share in common, such as direct labor hours or direct labor cost. The common characteristic is referred to as an **allocation base**.

An **overhead allocation rate** is calculated by dividing estimated overhead cost by the estimated quantity of the allocation base. For example, suppose a company anticipates $200,000 of manufacturing overhead and 25,000 direct labor hours during the year. The overhead allocation rate of $8 ($200,000 ÷ 25,000) indicates that each job will be assigned $8 of overhead for every direct labor hour worked. The amount of overhead assigned to jobs is referred to as **overhead applied**.

Recording manufacturing overhead is a two-step process. First, when actual overhead costs are incurred, the Manufacturing Overhead account is debited (increased). Second, when overhead is applied to jobs, the Manufacturing Overhead account is credited (decreased), and the Work in Process Inventory account is debited (increased). The journal entry to record step one is:

Manufacturing Overhead	XXX	
Various accounts		XXX

The journal entry to record step two is:

Work in Process Inventory	XXX	
Manufacturing Overhead		XXX

When jobs are completed, Work in Process is reduced (credited) and Finished Goods is increased (debited). The appropriate entry is:

Finished Goods	XXX	
Work in Process		XXX

When completed jobs are sold, Finished Goods is reduced (credited) by the cost of the completed jobs and the Cost of Goods Sold account is increased (debited). The appropriate entry is:

Cost of Goods Sold	XXX	
Finished Goods Inventory		XXX

Overhead allocation is the process of assigning manufacturing overhead to specific jobs and recording overhead in various accounts. As mentioned earlier, overhead costs are allocated to jobs by means of an overhead allocation rate, calculated as the ratio of estimated overhead costs to estimated level of activity. The allocation base (activity such as direct labor cost or machine hours) should be strongly associated with overhead costs. That is, increases in overhead cost should coincide with increases in the allocation base.

Activity-based costing (ABC) is a method of assigning overhead costs to products using a number of different allocation bases. Major activities that create overhead costs are identified. The costs of the major activities are grouped into **cost pools**. Multiple overhead rates are calculated by dividing the amount of each cost pool by a measure of its corresponding activity (referred to as a **cost driver**). Overhead is then assigned to a job based on how much of each activity it caused.

LO7   *Explain the role of a predetermined overhead rate in applying overhead to jobs.*

Overhead rates can be developed by dividing actual overhead by the actual level of the allocation base. However, because total actual overhead cost and the total actual level of the allocation base are not known until the end of the accounting period, most companies do not use this method. An immediate cost figure may be needed so a company can determine the price to charge a customer and to determine the profitability or jobs.

Overhead rates are typically based on estimates of overhead cost and estimates of the level of the allocation base. Overhead rates based on these estimated figures are referred to as **predetermined overhead rates**.

$$\text{Predetermined overhead rate} \ = \ \frac{\text{Estimated total overhead cost}}{\text{Estimated level of allocation base}}$$

LO8   *Explain why the difference between actual overhead and overhead allocated to jobs using a predetermined rate is closed to Cost of Goods Sold or is apportioned among Work in Process Inventory, Finished Goods Inventory, and Cost of Goods Sold.*

As previously stated, recording manufacturing overhead is a two-step process. First, the actual cost of various overhead items are accumulated in the Manufacturing Overhead account. Second, overhead is applied to individual jobs using the predetermined overhead rate, which increases the Work in Process account and decreases the Manufacturing Overhead account. In step one, the debit entries to the Manufacturing Overhead account record actual overhead costs incurred and in step two, the credit entries to the Manufacturing Overhead account record the amount of overhead applied to jobs in process.

Because the predetermined overhead rate is based on estimated costs and level of activity, there is likely to be a difference between the debits to manufacturing overhead (recording actual overhead costs) and the credits to manufacturing overhead (recording the amount of overhead applied to jobs during the period using the predetermined overhead rate). The difference is referred to as **underapplied overhead** if actual overhead is greater than the amount of overhead applied and as **overapplied overhead** if actual overhead is less than the amount applied.

At the end of the accounting period, under- or overapplied overhead is equal to the balance in Manufacturing Overhead and must be closed. If the amount of over- or underapplied overhead is not large, most companies simply close the Manufacturing Overhead account and adjust the Cost of Goods Sold account.

Theoretically, the amount of under- or overhead applied overhead should be apportioned among Work in Process, Finished Goods, and Cost of Goods Sold. Because the cost of jobs is reflected in Work in Process, Finished Goods, and Cost of Goods Sold, all these accounts should be adjusted to reflect actual overhead costs. Apportioning the over- or under applied overhead can be accomplished based on the relative cost recorded in these accounts.

Many service companies use job-order costing. For example, a hospital might want to know the cost of treating a patient. Therefore, the patient becomes a "job." Costs are accumulated on a report much like a job-cost sheet used in a manufacturing setting.

LO9 *Discuss changes in manufacturing practices and how they affect product costing*

In the last two decades, many U.S. manufacturers have made fundamental changes in their operations and business philosophies in order to compete effectively in a global economy. Three of the major changes are discussed in this chapter: just-in-time production, computer-controlled manufacturing, and total quality management.

A **just-in-time (JIT)** system is an innovative manufacturing system first used by Japanese companies. One important goal of a JIT system is to minimize inventories of raw materials and work in process. Companies with JIT systems make arrangements with suppliers to deliver materials just before they are needed in the production process. Production lines are scheduled just in time to meet the requirements of the next production line. JIT is more than an effort to reduce inventories. The goals of a JIT system are to develop a balanced production system that is flexible and allows for smooth, rapid flow of materials. JIT systems concentrate on improving quality, eliminating production breakdowns, and preventing missed delivery deadlines by suppliers.

More and more companies are using highly automated **computer-controlled manufacturing systems**. Using computers to control equipment, including robots, generally increases the flexibility and accuracy of the production process. State-of-the-art equipment and computer control systems have a significant effect on the composition of product costs. Drastic decreases in labor costs have been reported by some highly automated companies. Investing in state-of-the-art equipment also changes the mix of fixed and variable costs. When equipment is substituted for labor, fixed costs generally increase, and variable costs decrease.

An increasing number of companies have instituted **total quality management (TQM)** programs to ensure that their products are of the highest quality and that production processes are efficient. Most companies with TQM develop a company philosophy that stresses listening to the needs of customers, making products right the first time and reducing defective products that must be reworked, and encouraging workers to continuously improve their production processes. TQM affects product costing by reducing the need to track the cost of scrap and rework related to each job.

Review of Key Terms

Activity-based costing: A method of assigning overhead costs that identifies key activities and accumulates the costs associated with them

Allocation base (cost driver): The measure of activity used to calculate an overhead rate.

Computer-controlled manufacturing system: A highly automated manufacturing system that uses computers to control equipment and generally increases the flexibility and accuracy of the production process.

Cost driver: A measure of the activity, related to a cost pool, that is used to allocate cost.

Cost of goods available for sale: The sum of the beginning balance in finished goods plus the cost of goods manufactured.

Cost of goods manufactured: The cost of items that have been completed in the current accounting period.

Cost pool: A grouping of overhead costs based on the major activity that created them. Also, a grouping of individual costs whose total is allocated using one allocation base.

Direct labor cost: Labor that is directly traced to items produced.

Direct material cost: Materials and parts that are directly traced to items produced.

Finished Goods Inventory: The costs of goods that are completed and ready to sell.

Full costing: An approach to product costing that includes direct material, direct labor and both fixed and variable manufacturing overhead in product cost.

General and administrative costs: Costs associated with the firm's general management.

Indirect labor costs: All labor costs that are not directly traced to items produced.

Indirect materials cost: Materials and parts that are not directly traced to items produced.

Job-cost sheet: A form used to accumulate the cost of producing an item for order or inventory.

Job-order costing system: A system of accounting for product cost used by companies that produce individual products or batches of unique products.

Just-in-time (JIT): A manufacturing system designed to minimize inventories of raw materials and work in process. In a JIT system, goods are manufactured just before sale and purchases are made just before goods are needed in production.

Manufacturing costs: All costs associated with the production of goods.

Manufacturing overhead: The costs of manufacturing activities other than direct material and direct labor.

Nonmanufacturing costs: Costs that are not associated with the production of goods.

Overapplied overhead: The excess of overhead applied to inventory using a predetermined rate over actual overhead.

Overhead allocation: The process of assigning overhead to specific costs objectives.

Overhead allocation rate: A measure of overhead cost divided by a measure of the overhead allocation base

Overhead applied: The amount of overhead assigned to jobs.

Period costs: Costs identified with accounting periods rather than with goods produced.

Predetermined overhead rate: The estimated level of overhead cost divided by the estimated level of the allocation base.

Process costing system: A product costing system used by companies that produce large numbers of identical items in a continuous production process.

Product costs: Costs assigned to goods produced.

Product costing system: An integrated set of documents, ledgers, accounts, and accounting procedures used to measure and record the cost of manufactured products.

Raw material inventory: An account that includes the cost of materials on hand that are used to produce a company's products.

Selling costs: Costs associated with securing and filling customer orders.

Time tickets: Forms completed by workers to keep track of the amount of time spent on each job.

Total quality management (TQM): Programs designed to ensure high-quality products that involve listening to customers' needs, making products right the first time, reducing defective products, and encouraging workers to improve their production processes continuously.

Underapplied overhead: The amount by which actual overhead exceeds the amount applied to inventory using a predetermined overhead rate.

Work in process inventory: An account that includes the cost of goods that are partially complete.

Chapter 2 – True/False

_F_   1.   Manufacturing costs include three cost categories: direct material, direct labor, and period costs.

_T_   2.   When finished goods are sold, the cost of the inventory sold is considered an expense and must be removed from Finished Goods Inventory and charged to Cost of Goods Sold.

_T_   3.   A ship building company would appropriately use a job-order costing system.

_F_   4.   An overhead allocation rate is calculated as the ratio of overhead costs to activity.

_F_   5.   Service companies do not use job-order costing systems.

_F_   6.   The two product costing systems are job-order costing and just-in-time.

_F_   7.   If actual overhead is less than the overhead applied, overhead is said to be under applied.

_T_   8.   A job is an individual product or batch for which a company needs cost information.

_T_   9.   In a manufacturing firm, the cost of goods available for sale is the sum of the beginning inventory balance in Finished Goods plus cost of goods manufactured.

_F_   10.   The costs of direct materials and direct labor are added to manufacturing overhead.

_F_   11.   A job cost sheet is used to request the release of materials from a company's storage area.

_T_   12.   The term full costs means that product cost includes both variable and fixed manufacturing overhead as well as direct material and direct labor, which are generally variable costs.

Chapter 2 – Key Terms Matching

Match the terms, found in Chapter 2, with the following definitions:

a. activity-based costing (ABC)
b. cost of goods manufactured
c. job cost sheet
d. job-order costing
e. just-in-time (JIT)
f. period costs

g. predetermined overhead rate
h. process costing
i. product costs
j. selling costs
k. underapplied overhead
l. work in process inventory

G 1. A rate obtained by dividing the estimated overhead by the estimated level of the allocation base

L 2. The inventory account for the cost of goods that are only partially completed

A 3. A method of assigning overhead costs to products using a number of different allocation bases

K 4. The difference if actual overhead is greater than the amount of overhead applied

J 5. Includes all the costs associated with securing and filling customer orders

E 6. An innovative manufacturing system that minimizes inventories

C 7. A form, typically computer generated, used to accumulate the cost of producing the item or items ordered

i 8. The costs assigned to goods produced; the manufacturing costs

B 9. The cost of the completed items

F 10. Costs that are identified with accounting periods rather than with goods produced

D 11. Costing systems used by companies that produce individual products or batches of products that are unique

h 12. Costing systems used by companies that produce large quantities of identical items.

Chapter 2 – Multiple Choice

1.   Which of the following would not be classified as a manufacturing cost?
      a.   Direct labor
      b.   Selling costs
      c.   Direct materials
      d.   Manufacturing overhead

2.   The cost incurred in maintaining the factory building and grounds is referred to as:
      a.   an administrative cost.
      b.   direct materials.
      c.   direct labor.
      d.   manufacturing overhead.

3.   Product costs can be thought of as all of the following except:
      a.   direct materials and direct labor.
      b.   manufacturing costs.
      c.   selling and administrative expenses.
      d.   indirect materials and indirect labor.

4.   Which of the following costs would not be included in direct materials for Eastlake Motorboat Company?
      a.   Wood
      b.   Steering assembly
      c.   Screws and glue
      d.   All of the above

5.   The inventory accounts for a manufacturing concern include:
      a.   raw materials, direct labor and manufacturing overhead.
      b.   raw materials, work in process and finished goods.
      c.   direct labor, selling expenses and administrative expenses.
      d.   raw materials, direct labor and administrative expenses.

6.   A job-cost sheet is typically a computerized form used to accumulate:
      a.   cost of raw materials purchased.
      b.   cost of goods sold.
      c.   actual overhead cost.
      d.   cost of direct materials, direct labor and manufacturing overhead.

7.   The method of applying overhead to products using a number of different allocation bases is called:
      a.   activity-based costing (ABC).
      b.   just in time (JIT).
      c.   predetermined overhead method.
      d.   total quality management (TQM).

8.   A number of companies have instituted total quality management to:
    a.   ensure that products are of the highest quality.
    b.   to ensure that production processes are efficient.
    c.   both a and b above.
    d.   none of the above.

9.   In a typical job-order costing system the costs charged to a job are:
    a.   actual direct materials, estimated direct labor, and estimated manufacturing overhead.
    b.   estimated direct materials, estimated direct labor, and estimated manufacturing overhead.
    c.   actual direct materials, actual direct labor, and actual manufacturing overhead.
    d.   actual direct materials, actual direct labor, and estimated manufacturing overhead.

10.   During the month of January the Terrill company had the following costs: direct materials $52,000; direct labor $48,500; indirect materials $16,000; indirect labor $5,600; selling expenses $15,000; general and administrative expenses $9,000; taxes on the factory building $2,000; and rent on the factory building $18,000. The beginning inventory in work in process was $18,000 and the ending inventory work in process was $19,000. The cost of goods manufactured for the month was:
    a. $142,100.
    b. $141,100.
    c. $156,100.
    d. $165,000.

11.   The predetermined overhead rate is computed by dividing:
    a.   actual total overhead cost by estimated level of allocation base.
    b.   estimated total overhead cost by estimated level of allocation base.
    c.   estimated total overhead cost by actual of allocation base.
    d.   none of the above.

12.   The Far and Away Corporation applies overhead to work in process based on machine hours. Far and Away estimated manufacturing overhead for the following period would be $450,000 and that machine hours would total 90,000. Assuming the actual manufacturing overhead was $447,500 and that actual machine totaled 87,000, manufacturing overhead was:
    a. $12,500 overapplied.
    b. $ 2,500 overapplied.
    c. $12,500 underapplied.
    d. $ 2,500 underapplied.

Exercise 2 – 1 Determine the missing amounts in each of the following cases:

	CASES		
	A	B	C
Direct materials	$ 69,000	410,000	$ 39,000
Direct labor	15,000	60,000	$11,000
Manufacturing overhead	47,150	350,000	73,000
Total manufacturing costs	131,150.00	820,000	$123,000
Beginning work in process inventory	4,000	90,000	40,000
Ending work in process inventory	5,000	60,000	32,000
Cost of goods manufactured	$130,150	850,000	$131,000
Sales	$200,000		$300,000
Beginning finished goods inventory	9,000		180,000
Cost of Goods manufactured	130,150	850,000	131,000
Goods available for sale		975,000	
Ending finished goods inventory	11,000		114,000
Cost of goods sold	128,150	800,000	
Gross margin		700,000	
Operating expenses	20,000		83,000
Net income		$150,000	$20,000

Exercise 2 – 2 Classify each of the following items as either a product cost or a period cost. Classify each of the costs further. For example, if the cost is a product cost indicate whether it is direct materials, direct labor, or manufacturing overhead. If the cost is a period cost, indicate whether it is a selling or administrative expense. Place an X in the appropriate column for each cost to indicate whether the cost would be a period cost or a product cost; materials, labor, or overhead; selling or administrative.

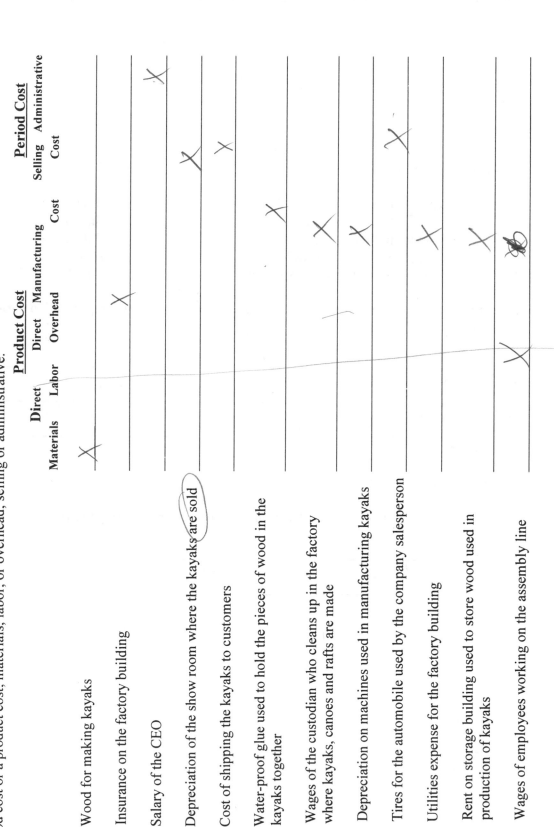

	Product Cost			Period Cost	
	Direct Materials	Direct Labor	Manufacturing Overhead Cost	Selling Cost	Administrative Cost
a. Wood for making kayaks	X				
b. Insurance on the factory building			X		
c. Salary of the CEO					X
d. Depreciation of the show room where the kayaks are sold				X	
e. Cost of shipping the kayaks to customers				X	
f. Water-proof glue used to hold the pieces of wood in the kayaks together			X		
g. Wages of the custodian who cleans up in the factory where kayaks, canoes and rafts are made			X		
h. Depreciation on machines used in manufacturing kayaks			X		
i. Tires for the automobile used by the company salesperson				X	
j. Utilities expense for the factory building			X		
k. Rent on storage building used to store wood used in production of kayaks			X		
l. Wages of employees working on the assembly line		X			

Exercise 2 – 3 The following costs and inventory data were taken from the Stoll Company accounts as of December 31, 2001.

	January 1, 2001 Beginning Inventory	December 31, 2001 Ending Inventory
Inventories:		
Raw materials	$ 20,000	$ 18,000
Work in process	24,000	30,000
Finished goods	17,000	15,000
Costs incurred:		
Purchase of raw materials		$ 120,000
Direct labor		90,000
Rent, factory		50,000
Utilities, factory		8,000
Indirect materials		14,000
Indirect labor		9,000
Selling expenses		12,000
Administrative expenses		17,000

1. Prepare a schedule showing the amount of direct materials used in production during the year.

_____

_____

_____

_____

2. Determine the amount of manufacturing overhead incurred during the year.

_____

_____

_____

_____

_____

Exercise 2 – 3 - Continued

3.   Using the information found in parts 1 and 2, prepare a schedule of Cost of Goods Manufactured for the year ending December 31, 2001 in good form.

_____

_____

_____

_____

_____

_____

_____

_____

_____

_____

_____

_____

_____

4.   Prepare the Cost of Goods Sold section of the Income Statement for Stoll Company for the year ending December 31, 2001 in good form.

_____

_____

_____

_____

_____

Problem 2 – 4 The Weisshorn Company puts a medium black cartridge in each ball point pen they manufacture. In June of the current year, Weisshorn bought 10,000 medium black cartridges at a cost of $2 each. During June, 80 percent of the cartridges were withdrawn from inventory. Two hundred of the 80 percent that were withdrawn from inventory were given to sales personnel to use in their personal pens. The remaining 7,800 cartridges were placed into pens being manufactured by the company. Of the pens in production during June, 85 percent were completed and transferred from work in process to finished goods. Of the pens completed during June, 30 percent of them were unsold as of June 30. There were no inventories of any type on June 1.

Determine the cost of cartridges in each of the following accounts as of June 30.

Raw materials   _____

Work in Process   _____

Finished Goods   _____

Cost of Goods Sold   _____

Selling Expenses   _____

Total   _____

Hint: Remember there are only 10,000 cartridges at a cost of $2 each. Therefore, your total should be $20,000.

Problem 2 – 5 The Third Pigg Brick Company manufactures custom bricks used in upscale homes. No two customers have the same type of bricks. The bricks go through three processes: mixing; shaping; and firing. The company uses a job-order cost system and computes a predetermined overhead rate in each department. The mixing department bases its rate on direct materials, the shaping department bases its rate on machine hours and the firing department bases its rate on direct labor hours. At the beginning of the year the company made the following estimates:

	Department		
	Mixing	**Shaping**	**Firing**
Direct labor hours	160,000	90,000	120,000
Machine hours	60,000	140,000	42,000
Direct materials cost	$600,000	$ 80,000	$ 30,000
Manufacturing overhead cost	$300,000	$280,000	$150,000

1. Compute the predetermined overhead rate to be used in each department during the upcoming year.

   Mixing_____

   Shaping_____

   Firing_____

2. Suppose the overhead rates you computed in (1) above are in effect. Compute the total overhead cost to be assigned to Ms. Snout's order – Job 332 assuming the following data:

	Department		
	Mixing	**Shaping**	**Firing**
Direct labor hours	300	80	92
Machine hours	80	120	120
Direct materials cost	$6,000	$120	$ 300

3. If actual overhead incurred totaled $3,500, compute the amount of over- or underapplied manufacturing overhead.

Solutions – Chapter 2 – True/False

1. F   Manufacturing cost include direct material, direct labor, and manufacturing overhead.
2. T
3. T
4. T
5. F   Many service companies (e.g., repair shops and consulting firms) use job-order costing
6. F   The two major product costing systems are job-order and process costing systems.
7. F   If actual overhead is less than the overhead applied, overhead is said to be overapplied.
8. T
9. T
10. F   Costs included in manufacturing overhead are indirect costs. Both direct materials and direct labor are direct costs.
11. F   A material requisition form is used to request the release of materials from a company's storage area.
12. T

Solutions – Chapter 2 – Key Terms Matching

1. g. predetermined overhead rate
2. l. work in Process Inventory
3. a. activity-based costing (ABC)
4. k. underapplied overhead
5. j. selling costs
6. e. just-in-time
7. c. job-cost sheet
8. i. product costs
9. b. cost of goods manufactured
10. f. period costs
11. d. job-order costing
12. h. process costing

Solutions – Chapter 2 – Multiple Choice

1. b
2. d
3. c
4. c
5. b
6. d
7. a
8. c
9. d
10. b
11. b
12. c

Solution – Exercise 2 – 1 Determine the missing amounts in each of the following cases:

CASES

	A	B	C
Direct materials	$ 69,000	$410,000	$ 39,000
Direct labor	15,000	60,000	11,000
Manufacturing overhead	47,150	350,000	73,000
Total manufacturing costs	131,150	820,000	123,000
Beginning work in process inventory	4.000	90,000	40,000
Ending work in process inventory	5,000	60,000	32,000
Cost of goods manufactured	$130,150	$850,000	$131,000
Sales	$200,000	$1,500,000	$300,000
Beginning finished goods inventory	9,000	125,000	180,000
Cost of Goods manufactured	130,150	850,000	131.000
Goods available for sale	139,150	975,000	311,000
Ending finished goods inventory	11,000	175,000	114,000
Cost of goods sold	128,150	800,000	197,000
Gross margin	71,850	700,000	103,000
Operating expenses	20,000	550,000	83,000
Net income	$ 51,850	$150,000	$ 20,000

Solution – Exercise 2 – 2

Solution – Exercise 2 – 2 Classify each of the following items as either a product cost or a period cost. Classify each of the costs further. For example, if the cost is a product cost indicate whether it is direct materials, direct labor or manufacturing overhead. If the cost is a period cost, indicate whether it is a selling or administrative expense. Place an X in the appropriate column for each cost to indicate whether the cost would be a period cost or a product cost; materials, labor, or overhead; selling or administrative.

	Product Cost			Period Cost	
	Direct Materials	Direct Labor	Manufacturing Overhead	Selling Cost	Administrative Cost
a. Wood for making kayaks	X				
b. Insurance on the factory building			X		
c. Salary of the CEO					X
d. Depreciation of the show room where the kayaks are sold				X	
e. Cost of shipping the kayaks to customers				X	
f. Water-proof glue used to hold the pieces of wood in the kayaks together			X		
g. Wages of the custodian who cleans up in the factory where kayaks, canoes and rafts are made			X		
h. Depreciation on the machines used in manufacturing kayaks			X		
i. Tires for the automobile used by the company salesperson				X	
j. Utilities expense for the factory building			X		
k. Rent on storage building used to store wood used in production			X		
l. Wages of employees working on the assembly line		X			

Solution − Exercise 2 − 3 - The following costs and inventory data were taken from the Stoll Company accounts as of December 31, 2001.

	January 1, 2001 Beginning Inventory	December 31, 2001 Ending Inventory
Inventories:		
Raw materials	$ 20,000	$ 18,000
Work in process	24,000	30,000
Finished goods	17,000	15,000
Costs incurred:		
Purchase of raw materials		$ 120,000
Direct labor		90,000
Rent, factory		50,000
Utilities, factory		8,000
Indirect materials		14,000
Indirect labor		9,000
Selling expenses		12,000
Administrative expenses		17,000

1.   Prepare a schedule showing the amount of direct materials used in production during the year.

Beginning balance Raw Materials Inventory	$ 20,000
Raw materials purchased	120,000
Raw materials available	140,000
Ending balance Raw Materials Inventory	18,000
Raw materials used in production	$122,000

2.   Determine the amount of manufacturing overhead incurred during the year.

Rent, factory	$50,000
Utilities, factory	8,000
Indirect materials	14,000
Indirect labor	9,000
Manufacturing overhead incurred	$81,000

Solution – Exercise 2 – 3 - Continued

3.   Using the information found in parts 1 and 2, prepare a schedule of Cost of Goods Manufactured for the year ending December 31, 2001 in good form.

Stoll Company
Schedule of Cost of Goods Manufactured
For the Year Ending December 31, 2001

Beginning balance in work in process			$ 24,000
Add: Current manufacturing costs			
Beginning balance Raw Materials Inventory	$ 20,000		
Raw materials purchased	120,000		
Raw materials available	140,000		
Ending balance Raw Materials Inventory	18,000		
Raw materials used in production		$122,000	
Direct labor		90,000	
Manufacturing overhead			
Rent, factory	$50,000		
Utilities, factory	8,000		
Indirect materials	14,000		
Indirect labor	9,000		
Manufacturing overhead incurred		81,000	293,000
Total			$317,000
Less: Ending balance work in process			30,000
Cost of goods manufactured			$287,000

4.   Prepare the Cost of Goods Sold section of the Income Statement for Stoll Company for the year ending December 31, 2001 in good form.

Cost of Goods Sold

Beginning balance finished goods	$ 17,000
Add: cost of goods manufactured	287,000
Cost of goods available for sale	$304,000
Less: ending finished goods	15,000
Cost of goods sold	$289,000

Solution — Problem 2 — 4 The Weisshorn Company puts a medium black cartridge in each ball point pen they manufacture. In June of the current year, Weisshorn bought 10,000 medium black cartridges at a cost of $2 each. During June 80 percent of the cartridges were withdrawn from inventory. Two hundred of the 80 percent that were withdrawn from inventory were given to sales personnel to use in their personal pens. The remaining 7,800 cartridges were placed into pens being manufactured by the company. Of the pens in production during June, 85 percent were completed and transferred from work in process to finished goods. Of the pens completed during June, 30 percent of them were unsold as of June 30. There were no inventories of any type on June 1.

Determine the cost of cartridges in each of the following accounts as of June 30.

Raw materials	$4,000	(10,000 - 8,000) x $2
Work in Process	2,340	(7,800 x .15) x $2
Finished Goods	3,978	[(7,800 x .85) x .30] x $2
Cost of Goods Sold	9,282	[7,800 x .85) x .70] x $2
Selling Expenses	400	200 x $2
Total	$20,000	

Solution – Problem 2 – 5

The Third Pigg Brick Company manufactures custom bricks used in upscale homes. No two customers have the same type of bricks. The bricks go through three processes: mixing; shaping; and firing. The company uses a job-order cost system and computes a predetermined overhead rate in each department. The mixing department bases its rate on direct materials, the shaping department bases its rate on machine hours and the firing department bases its rate on direct labor hours. At the beginning of the year the company made the following estimates:

	Department		
	Mixing	**Shaping**	**Firing**
Direct labor hours	160,000	90,000	120,000
Machine hours	60,000	140,000	42,000
Direct materials cost	$600,000	$ 80,000	$ 30,000
Manufacturing overhead cost	$300,000	$280,000	$150,000

1. Compute the predetermined overhead rate to be used in each department during the upcoming year.

    Mixing $300,000/$600,000 = 50% Direct Materials Cost

    Shaping $280,000/140 Machine Hours = $2 per MH

    Firing $150,000/120,000 Direct Labor Hours = $1.25 per DLH

2. Suppose the overhead rates you computed in (1) above are in effect. Compute the total overhead cost to be assigned to Ms. Snout's order – Job 332 assuming the following data:

	Department		
	Mixing	**Shaping**	**Firing**
Direct labor hours	300	80	92
Machine hours	80	120	120
Direct materials cost	$6,000	$120	$ 300

    Mixing - $6,000 × .50 = $3,000

    Shaping - 120 MH × $2 =   240

    Firing -   92 × $1.25 =   115

    Total $3,355

3. If actual overhead incurred totaled $3,500, compute the amount of over- or underapplied manufacturing overhead.

    Actual overhead $3,500
    Overhead applied   3,355
    Underapplied overhead $ 145

CHAPTER 3

PROCESS COSTING

CHAPTER INTRODUCTION

There are two primary systems for calculating the cost of inventory: a job-order costing system and a process costing system. In a job-order costing system, each unique product is a "job" for which the company needs cost information. Thus, it is necessary to trace manufacturing costs to these specific jobs. When jobs are completed, the cost of the jobs is removed from Work in Process Inventory and added to Finished Goods Inventory. When completed jobs are sold, the cost of the jobs is removed from Finished Goods Inventory and added to Cost of Goods Sold.

This chapter describes a process costing system, which is essentially a system of averaging. Dividing production costs by the total number of homogeneous items produced results in an average cost per unit. When items are completed, multiplying the number of units completed by the average unit cost determines the cost to remove from Work in Process Inventory and add to Finished Goods Inventory. When items are sold, multiplying the number of units sold by the average unit cost determines the cost to remove from Finished Goods Inventory and add to Cost of Goods Sold.

Objectives, Terms, and Discussions.

LO1   *Describe how products flow through departments and how costs flow through accounts.*

When a company uses process costing, a product typically passes through two or more departments. Generally, identifying the stage when materials enter the production process is easy. However, determining exactly when labor and overhead are added to the process is more difficult. Labor and overhead are often grouped together and referred to as **conversion costs**. These costs are often assumed to enter the process evenly throughout the process.

The product costs accumulated in a process costing system are essentially the same costs considered in a job-order costing system: direct material, direct labor, and manufacturing overhead. In addition, a processing department may have a cost called **transferred-in cost**. This is a cost incurred in one processing department that is transferred to the next processing department.

Each processing department accumulates product cost in a separate departmental Work in Process account. The following entries illustrate the flow of costs between processing departments:

Assume that $160,000 of direct material is used during the month in Department A:

Work in Process, Department A	$160,000	
Raw Materials Inventory		$160,000

Assume that $40,000 of direct labor cost is incurred during the month in Department A:

Work in Process, Department A	$40,000	
Wages Payable		$40,000

Many companies use a predetermined overhead rate to assign overhead to Work in Process. Assume that at the beginning of the year, Department A estimates it will incur $1,000,000 of overhead cost and $400,000 of direct labor cost. Using direct labor cost as an allocation base, Department A calculates a predetermined overhead rate of 250 percent for each direct labor dollar incurred. If $40,000 of direct labor costs were incurred during the current month, $100,000 ($40,000 × 2.50) of overhead would be assigned to Work in Process, Department A:

Work in Process, Department A	$100,000	
Manufacturing Overhead		$100,000

The cost of items transferred from one department to the next is referred to as transferred-in cost. Suppose that during the month, Department A completes units with a cost of $299,000 and transfers the units to Department B. The entry to record the transfer is:

Work in Process, Department B	$299,000	
Work in Process, Department A		$299,000

LO2   *Discuss the concept of an equivalent unit.*

In calculating the average unit cost, it is necessary to take into account the number of partially completed units in work in process in terms of an equivalent number of whole units. When partially completed units are converted to a comparable number of completed units, they are referred to as **equivalent units**. For example, if 100 units in work in process are 25 percent completed, then they are equivalent to 25 whole units (100 × 25%). The number of equivalent units in work in process may be different for material and conversion costs because material and conversion costs enter the production process at different times.

LO3   *Calculate the cost per equivalent unit.*

The average cost in a process costing system is referred to as cost per equivalent unit. The formula for calculating the cost per equivalent unit is:

$$\text{Cost per equivalent unit} = \frac{\text{Cost in beginning WIP} + \text{Costs incurred in current period}}{\text{Units completed} + \text{Equivalent units in ending WIP}}$$

LO4 *Calculate the cost of goods completed and the ending Work in Process balance in a processing department.*

An example demonstrates the application of cost per equivalent units. Suppose at the beginning of the period, Department A has on hand beginning work in process inventory consisting of 8,000 units that are 70 percent complete. During the period 50,000 units are started and 46,000 units are completed. At the end of the month, 12,000 units are on hand that are 40 percent complete as to conversion costs. The cost in beginning Work in Process, Department A consists of $14,000 of material cost, $10,800 of labor cost, and $27,000 of overhead cost. During the period, Department A incurs $160,000 of material cost and $40,000 of labor cost. The predetermined overhead rate is $2.50 for each dollar of direct labor cost. Therefore $100,000 (2.50 × $40,000) of overhead is applied to production during the period. The cost per equivalent unit for Department B is as follows:

Cost	Material	Labor	Overhead	Total
Beginning WIP	$ 14,000	$10,800	$ 27,000	$ 51,800
Current period cost	160,000	40,000	100,000	300,000
Total Cost	$174,000	$50,800	$127,000	$351,800

Units				
Units completed	46,000	46,000	46,000	
Equivalent units,				
Ending WIP	12,000*	4,800**	4,800**	
Total units	58,000	50,800	50,800	

*12,000 whole units x 100 percent; **12,000 whole units x 40 percent

Cost per equivalent unit
(total cost/total units) $3.00   + $1.00   + $2.50   = $6.50

The 46,000 units that are competed are transferred to Department B. The cost is $299,000 (46,000 units × $6.50 per unit). The entry to record the transfer is:

Work in Process, Department B $299,000
      Work in Process, Department A $299,000

The ending balance in Work in Process, Department A is $52,800 [(12,000 × $3 of material) + (4,800 × $1 of labor) + (4,800 × $2.50 of overhead)].

LO5 *Describe a production cost report.*

A production cost report is an end-of-the-month report for a process costing system that provides a reconciliation of units and costs as well as details of the cost per equivalent unit calculations. These reconciliations help ensure that mistakes are not made in calculations.

Assuming no loss of units, the number of units in beginning Work in Process Inventory plus the number of units started during the period will be equal to the number of units completed plus the number of units in ending Work in Process Inventory. In the previous example, Department A had 8,000 units in beginning Work in Process Inventory and 50,000 units were started, which means that 58,000 units must be accounted for as completed or remaining in ending work in process inventory. Since 46,000 units were completed and transferred to Department B and 12,000 units remained in ending Work in Process Inventory, all the units are accounted for. Department A had $51,800 of cost in beginning Work in Process Inventory and $300,000 was added during the period, which means that $351,800 must be accounted for. Since $299,000 was transferred to Department B and $52,800 remained in ending Work in Process Inventory, all the $351,800 has been accounted for.

There are four basic steps in process costing.

- Step One accounts for the number of physical units. This is the number of physical units in work in process at the beginning of the period plus the number of units started during the period. This should equal the number of units completed and transferred to the next department or to Finished Goods Inventory plus the units remaining in ending Work in Process Inventory.
- Step Two calculates the cost per equivalent unit for material and conversion costs. The numerator includes the cost in beginning Work in Process plus the cost incurred during the month for material, labor and overhead. The denominator includes the number of units completed plus the number of equivalent units in ending Work in Process Inventory.
- Step Three assigns cost to items completed and items remaining in ending Work in Process Inventory. The cost of completed items is the number of units completed multiplied by the total cost per unit (from Step 2). The cost remaining in ending Work in Process is the sum of the products of equivalent units in process and cost per equivalent unit for material, labor, and overhead.
- Step Four reconciles the amount of product cost. The cost of beginning Work in Process Inventory plus the cost incurred during the period should equal the amount of cost assigned to completed items plus the amount of cost assigned to ending Work in Process Inventory.

Review of Key Terms

Conversion costs: The total cost of labor and overhead.

Cost per equivalent unit: The sum of the cost in beginning work in process and the cost incurred in the current period divided by the sum of the units completed and the equivalent units in ending work in process.

Equivalent units: Partially completed units expressed as a comparable number of whole units.

Production cost report: A report in a process costing system that provides a reconciliation of units and a reconciliation of costs as well as the details of the cost per equivalent unit calculations.

Transferred-in cost: The cost a prior processing department incurs and transfers to the next processing department.

Chapter 3 – True/False

(T) F   1.   The two primary systems for calculating the cost of inventory are process costing and job function costing.
Job order costing

T   2.   Process costing is essentially a system of averaging.

T   3.   An example of a firm using a process costing system is Kimberly-Clark Corp.

F   4.   In a process costing system, multiplying the number of units completed by the average unit cost determines the cost to remove from Work in Process and include in Cost of Goods Sold.

T   5.   The product costs accumulated in a process costing system are essentially the same costs considered in a job-order costing system. *DL, DM, MOVOH.*

F   6.   When a processing department completes items, they are transferred to the next department along with the related costs. This cost is called prior department cost.

F   7.   The number of equivalent units in work in process is always the same for materials and conversion costs.

T   8.   In the formula for determining cost per equivalent unit, the numerator contains the costs in beginning Work in Process plus the costs incurred in the current period.

F   9.   A production cost report provides a reconciliation of only costs.

T   10.   In a production cost report, for each period the total costs to be accounted for is the sum of the beginning Work in Process and the costs incurred during the period.

T   11.   The cost of beginning Work in Process Inventory plus the costs incurred during the period should equal the amount of costs assigned to completed items plus the amount of costs assigned to items in ending Work in Process Inventory.

T   12.   Step 1 in process costing is to account for the number of physical units.

Chapter 3 - Key Terms Matching

Match the terms, found in Chapter 3, with the following definitions:

a. Conversion costs
b. Cost per equivalent unit
c. Equivalent units

d. Production cost report
e. Transferred-in cost

_____C_____ 1. Partially completed units converted to a comparable number of completed units

_____E_____ 2. A cost incurred in one processing department that is transferred to the next processing department

_____D_____ 3. An end-of-the-month report for a process costing system that provides a reconciliation of units and a reconciliation of costs as well as the details of the cost per equivalent unit calculations

_____B_____ 4. The average unit cost in a process costing system

_____A_____ 5. Labor and overhead

Chapter 3 – Multiple Choice

1.   Process costing is:
    a.   essentially a process of averaging.
    b.   used by a company producing large numbers of homogenous items in a continuous production process.
    c.   both a and b above.
    d.   none of the above.

2.   Conversion costs consist of:
    a.   direct labor.
    b.   direct labor and manufacturing overhead.
    c.   direct materials and direct labor.
    d.   direct materials, direct labor and manufacturing overhead.

3.   The product costs accumulated in a process costing system are:
    a.   essentially the same costs considered in job-order costing.
    b.   direct materials, direct labor and manufacturing overhead.
    c.   both a and b above.
    d.   none of the above.

4.   Equivalent units are:
    a.   used in job-order costing.
    b.   used in process costing.
    c.   partially completed units which have been converted to a comparable number of completed units.
    d.   both b and c above.

5.   The primary document in process costing is:
    a.   income statement.
    b.   statement of cash flows.
    c.   job cost sheet.
    d.   production cost report.

6.   The Smell Good Company of Paris, France produces an expensive perfume that goes through three departments – A, B, and C. Assume Department A has 60,000 liters in the beginning work in process. An additional 340,000 liters were added into production. The ending work in process inventory totaled 80,000 liters. How many liters were transferred to the next department?
    a.   260,000
    b.   400,000
    c.   320,000
    d.   none of the above.

7.   Process costing would be used by all of the following except a:
    a.   manufacturer of cereal.
    b.   builder of custom boats.
    c.   manufacturer of paper cups.
    d.   soft drink bottling plant.

8. A production cost report:
   a. is an end of the month report for a process costing system.
   b. provides a reconciliation of units and a reconciliation of costs.
   c. provides details of the cost per equivalent unit calculations.
   (d.) all of the above.

9. In a process costing system, costs are accumulated:
   a. by job.
   b. by processing department.
   c. by jobs and processing departments.
   d. none of the above.

The following data are to be used in answering 10 and 11.

The Simpson Glove Company uses a process costing system to account for the cost of manufacturing gloves. The gloves go through two departments, Cutting and Assembly. The Assembly Department started the month with 10,000 pairs of gloves in beginning Work in Process Inventory that were 80 % complete with respect to conversion costs. An additional 30,000 pairs of gloves were transferred from Cutting to Assembly. At the end of the month there were 12,000 pairs of gloves in the ending Work in Process Inventory of the Assembly Department that were 75% with respect to conversion costs.

10. How many pairs of gloves were transferred to finished goods during the month?
    a. 10,000
    b. 28,000
    c. 30,000
    d. 40,000

11. What were the equivalent units of production for conversion costs in the Assembly Department for the month?
    a. 28,000
    b. 12,000 $28 + 9 = 37,000$
    c. 37,000
    d. 40,000

12. There are four steps in solving a process costing problem. The order in which the steps hould be undertaken is:
    a. (1) reconciling the physical number of units, (2) calculate the cost per equivalent unit, (3) assign cost to items completed and items in ending Work in Process, and (4) account for the amount of product cost – the cost of beginning inventory plus the amount of cost incurred during the period.
    b. (1) calculate the cost per equivalent unit, (2) assign cost to items completed and items in ending Work in Process, (3) account for the amount of product cost – the cost of beginning inventory plus the amount of cost incurred during the period, and (4) reconciling the physical number of units.
    c. (1) account for the amount of product cost – the cost of beginning inventory plus the amount of cost incurred during the period (2) calculate the cost per equivalent unit, (3) assign cost to items completed and items in ending Work in Process, and (4) reconciling the physical number of units.
    d. none of the above

Exercise 3 –1 The Cutting Department of Forrest Corporation uses a process costing system. Materials are added at the beginning of the process and conversion costs are incurred uniformly throughout the assembly process. On December 1, 2004, the Cutting Department had 10,000 units that were 50 percent complete. During December the department added 70,000 units into production. On December 31, the Cutting Department had 14,000 units in ending work in process that were 40 percent complete with respect to labor and overhead.

1. Prepare a Unit Reconciliation schedule of a Production Cost Report for the Forrest Corporation.

Units in Beginning WIP	10,000 50%
Units started during December	70,000
Units to account for	80,000
Units completed and transferred to Sewing	66,000
Units in Ending WIP	14,000 40% (L + ov)
Units accounted for	80,000

2. Compute total equivalent units for materials and for conversion costs for the Cutting Department for January.

Units	Materials	Labor	Overhead
Units completed	66,000	66,000	66,000
EU, ending WIP	14,000	5,600	5,600
Total units	80,000	71,600	71,600

Exercise 3 – 2 Stoll, Inc. produces an organic shampoo that goes through two processes – blending and packaging. Complete the Cost Reconciliation section of the May, 2003 Production Cost Report for the Blending Department of Stoll, Inc.

Production Cost Report
Blending Department
May 2003

Unit Reconciliation

Units in Beginning WIP	8,000
Units started during May	52,000
Units to account for	60,000
Units completed and transferred	45,000
Units in Ending WIP	15,000
Units accounted for	60,000

Cost per Equivalent Unit Calculation

	Material	Labor	Overhead	Total
Cost				
Beginning WIP	$ 5,800	$ 7,056	$ 1,360	$ 14,216
Cost incurred – May	95,000	130,200	64,000	289,200
Total	$100,800	$137,256	$65,360	$303,416
Units				
Units completed	58,000	58,000	58,000	
EU end WIP	9,200	7,360	7,360	
Total	67,200	65,360	65,360	
Cost per equivalent unit	$1.50	$2.10	$1.00	$4.60

Cost Reconciliation

Total cost to account for $303,416

Cost of completed units (58,000 @ 4.6)   266,800
Cost of ending WIP
  Materials (9,200 @ 1.5)   13,800

  Labor (7,360 @ 2.10)   15,456

  Overhead (7,360 @ 1)   7,360   33,616

Total cost accounted for $303,416

Exercise 3 – 3 The Ralph Company, Ltd. buys wood that is used as a direct material in the production of polo mallets. After work is completed in the Shaping Department, mallets are transferred to the Finishing Department where a sealant is applied. Direct materials are added at the beginning of the process while conversion costs are incurred uniformly throughout the process. During the month of June the following cost were incurred in the Shaping Department:

Direct Materials	$1,200
Labor	1,900
Overhead	760
Total	*$3,860*

During June, the first month of operation, the Shaping Department started a total of 1,000 units, of which a total of 750 were completed during the month. The remaining 250, which were in work in process on June 30, were 80 percent complete with respect to conversion costs.

1. Prepare a Unit Reconciliation schedule for the Ralph Company.

Units in Beginning WIP	_____
Units started during June	_1,000_
Units to account for	_1,000_
Units completed and transferred to Finishing	_750_
Units in Ending WIP	_250_ — 80% (L+OH)
Units accounted for	_1,000_

2. Compute total equivalent units for materials and for conversion costs for the Shaping Department for June.

Units	Materials	Labor	Overhead
Units completed	750	750	750
EU, ending WIP	250	200	200
Total units	1000	950	950

Exercise 3 – 3 Continued

3.   Compute the cost per unit for materials and conversion.

	Material	Labor	Overhead	Total
Cost				
Beginning WIP				
Cost incurred – June	1,200,000	1,700,000	760	3860
Total	1,200,000	1,900000	760,000	3,810,000
Units				
Units completed				
EU, End WIP				
Total				
Cost per equivalent unit	1.2	2.0	2.0	5.2

4.   Complete a cost reconciliation schedule.

Cost Reconciliation

Total cost to account for   3860

Cost of completed units (_____ @ _____)   _____
Cost of ending WIP
   Materials (_____ @ _____)   _____

   Labor (_____ @ _____)   _____

   Overhead (_____ @ _____)   _____   _____

Total cost accounted for   _____

Problem 3 – 4 The Michael Company manufacturers a product that goes through two departments. During the month of May the following data were recorded for the Mixing Department:

	Units	Materials	Labor	Overhead
Units in Beginning WIP	8,000	$ 80,000	$ 32,000	$ 8,000
Units started during May	52,000			
Units transferred	45,000			
Units in Ending WIP	15,000			
Costs added during May		205,000	400,000	100,000

The ending work in process was 80 percent complete with respect to materials and 60 percent complete with respect to labor and overhead. Prepare a Production Cost Report for May.

Production Cost Report
Mixing Department
May 2003

Unit Reconciliation

Units in Beginning WIP	8,000
Units started during May	52,000
Units to account for	60,000
Units completed and transferred	45,000
Units in Ending WIP	15,000 → } 80% M
Units accounted for	60,000 } 60% L+OH

Cost per Equivalent Unit Calculation

	Material	Labor	Overhead	Total
Cost Beginning WIP	80	32	8	120
Cost incurred – May	205	400	100	705
Total	285	432	108	825

Units

	Material	Labor	Overhead
Units completed	45,000	45000	45,000
EU, WIP	12,000	9,000	9,000
Total	57,000	54,000	54,000
Cost per EU	5	8	2	$15

Cost Reconciliation

Total cost to account for   ═══════

Cost of completed units (_____ @ _____)   _____
Cost of ending WIP
  Materials (_____ @ _____)   _____

  Labor (_____ @ _____)   _____

  Overhead (_____ @ _____)   _____   _____

Total cost accounted for   ═══════

Problem 3 – 5 The Punt Company manufactures footballs used by a large number of NFL, AFL and collegiate football teams. The footballs go through two processes – cutting and molding. Punt experienced the following activity in its Molding Department during the month of November.

Units:

Units in Beginning WIP	5,000
Transferred in from Cutting Department during November	45,000
Completed during November	38,000

Costs:

Work in process, October 30	$	54,000*
Transferred from Cutting Department during November		624,995
Direct materials added during November		136,120
Conversion costs added during November		344,685

*The October 30 balance in WIP ($54,000) consists of transferred in costs, $30,405; direct materials costs, $6,680; and conversion costs $16,915.

Complete the following Production Cost Report.

Production Cost Report
Molding Department
November 2003

Unit Reconciliation

Units in Beginning WIP	5,000
Units started during November	45,000
Units to account for	50,000
Units completed and transferred	38,000
Units in Ending WIP (80% materials, 60% Conversion)	12,000
Total units to account for	50,000

Cost per Equivalent Unit Calculation

Cost	Material	Conversion	Trans.-In	Total
Beginning WIP	6,680	16,915	30,405	54,000
Cost incurred – Nov	136,120	344,685	624,995	1,105,800
Total	142,800	361,599	655,400	1,159,799
Units				
Units completed	38,000	38,000	38,000	
EU, End WIP	9,600	7,2		
Total	47,600	45,200		
Cost per EU				

Solutions – True/False

1. F The two primary systems for calculating the cost of inventory are process costing and job-order costing systems.
2. T
3. T
4. F In a process costing system, multiplying the number of units completed by the average unit cost determines the cost to remove from work in process and include in finished goods inventory.
5. T
6. F When one processing department completes its work, the items are transferred to the next department along with the related costs. This cost is referred to as transferred-n costs.
7. F The number of equivalent in work in process may be different for material and conversion costs because material and conversion costs enter the production process at different times.
8. T
9. F A production cost report provides a reconciliation of units and costs.
10. T
11. T
12. T

Solutions – Key Terms Matching

1. c. equivalent units
2. e. transferred-in cost
3. d production cost report

4. b. cost per equivalent unitt
5. a. conversion costs

Solutions – Multiple Choice

1. c
2. b
3. c
4. d
5. d
6. c

7. b
8. d
9. b
10. b
11. c
12. a

Solution – Exercise 3 – 1 The Cutting Department of Forrest Corporation uses a process costing system. Materials are added at the beginning of the process and conversion costs are incurred uniformly throughout the assembly process. On December 1, 2004, the Cutting Department had 10,000 units that were 50 percent complete. During December the department added 70,000 units into production. On December 31, the Cutting Department had 14,000 units in ending work in process that were 40 percent complete with respect to labor and overhead.

1.   Prepare a Unit Reconciliation schedule of a Production Cost Report for the Forrest Corporation.

Units in Beginning WIP	10,000
Units started during December	70,000
Units to account for	80,000
Units completed and transferred to Sewing	66,000
Units in Ending WIP	14,000
Units accounted for	80,000

2.   Compute total equivalent units for materials and for conversion costs for the Cutting Department for January.

Units	Materials	Labor	Overhead
Units completed	66,000	66,000	66,000
EU, ending WIP	14,000	5,600	5,600
Total units	80,000	71,600	71,600

Solution – Exercise 3 – 2
Stoll, Inc. produces an organic shampoo that goes through two processes – blending and packaging. Complete the Cost Reconciliation section of the May 2003 Production Cost Report for the Blending Department of Stoll, Inc.

Production Cost Report
Blending Department
May 2003

Unit Reconciliation

Units in Beginning WIP	8,000
Units started during May	52,000
Units to account for	60,000
Units completed and transferred	45,000
Units in Ending WIP	15,000
Units accounted for	60,000

Cost per Equivalent Unit Calculation

	Material	Labor	Overhead	Total
Cost				
Beginning WIP	$ 5,800	$ 7,056	$ 1,360	$ 14,216
Cost incurred – May	95,000	130,200	64,000	289,200
Total	$100,800	$137,256	$65,360	$303,416
Units				
Units completed	58,000	58,000	58,000	
EU end WIP	9,200	7,360	7,360	
Total	67,200	65,360	65,360	
Cost per equivalent unit	$1.50	$2.10	$1.00	$4.60

Cost Reconciliation

Total cost to account for			$303,416
Cost of completed units (58,000 @ $4.60)		266,800	
Cost of ending WIP			
Materials (9,200 @ $1.50)	$13,800		
Labor (7,360 @ $2.10)	15,456		
Overhead (7,360 @ $1.00)	7,360	36,616	
Total cost accounted for			$303,416

Solution – Exercise 3 – 3

The Ralph Company, Ltd. buys wood that is used as a direct material in the production of polo mallets. After work is completed in the Shaping Department mallets are transferred to the Finishing Department where a sealant is applied. Direct materials are added at the beginning of the process while conversion costs are incurred uniformly throughout the process. During the month of June the following cost were incurred in the Shaping Department:

Direct Materials	$1,200
Labor	1,900
Overhead	760

During June, the first month of operation, the Shaping Department started a total of 1,000 units, of which a total of 750 were completed during the month. The remaining 250, which were in work in process on June 30, were 80 percent complete with respect to conversion costs.

1. Prepare a Unit Reconciliation schedule for the Ralph Company.

Units in Beginning WIP	- 0 -
Units started during June	1,000
Units to account for	1,000
Units completed and transferred to Finishing	750
Units in Ending WIP	250
Units accounted for	1,000

2. Compute total equivalent units for materials and for conversion costs for the Shaping Department for June.

Units	Materials	Labor	Overhead
Units completed	750	750	750
EU, End WIP	250	200	200
Total units	1,000	950	950

3. Compute the cost per unit for materials and conversion.

	Material	Labor	Overhead	Total
Cost				
Beginning WIP	- 0 -	- 0 -	- 0 -	- 0 -
Cost incurred – June	$1,200	$1,900	$ 760	$3,860
Total	$1,200	$1,900	$ 760	$3,860
Units				
Units completed	750	750	750	
EU, End WIP	250	200	200	
Total	1,000	950	950	
Cost per EU	$1.20	$2.00	$ .80	$4.00

4. Complete a cost reconciliation schedule.

Reconciliation

Total cost to account for			$3,860
Cost of completed units	750 @ $4	$3,000	
Cost of ending WIP			
Materials (250 @ $1.20)		300	
Labor (200 @ $2)		400	
Overhead (200 @ $ .80)		160	860
Total cost accounted for			$3,860

Solution – Problem 3 – 4

Solution – Problem 3 – 4 The Michael Company manufacturers a product that goes through two departments. During the month of May the following data were recorded for the Mixing Department:

	Units	Materials	Labor	Overhead
Units in Beginning WIP	8,000	$ 80,000	$ 32,000	$ 8,000
Units started during May	52,000			
Units transferred	45,000			
Units in Ending WIP	15,000			
Costs added during May		205,000	400,000	100,000

The ending work in process was 80 percent complete with respect to materials and 60 percent complete with respect to labor and overhead. Prepare a Production Cost Report for May.

Production Cost Report
Mixing Department
May 2003

Unit Reconciliation

Units in Beginning WIP	8,000
Units started during May	52,000
Units to account for	60,000
Units completed and transferred	45,000
Units in Ending WIP	15,000
Units accounted for	60,000

Cost per Equivalent Unit Calculation

	Material	Labor	Overhead	Total
Cost				
Beginning WIP	$ 80,000	$ 32,000	$ 8,000	$120,000
Cost incurred – May	205,000	400,000	100,000	705,000
Total	$285,000	$432,000	$108,000	$825,000
Units				
Units completed	45,000	45,000	45,000	
EU, End WIP	12,000	9,000	9,000	
Total	57,000	54,000	54,000	
Cost per EU	$5.00	$8.00	$2.00	$15.00

Cost Reconciliation

Total cost to account for		$825,000
Cost of completed units (45,000 @ $15)	$675,000	
Cost of ending WIP		
Materials (12,000 @ $5)	$60,000	
Labor (9,000 @ $8)	72,000	
Overhead (9,000 @ $2)	18,000	150,000
Total cost accounted for		$825,000

Solution – Problem 3 – 5 The Punt Company manufactures footballs used by a large number of NFL, AFL and collegiate football teams. The footballs go through two processes – cutting and molding. Punt Company experienced the following activity in its Molding Department during the month of November.

Units:

Units in Beginning WIP	5,000
Transferred in from Cutting Department during November	45,000
Completed during November	38,000

Costs:

Work in process, October 30	$ 54,000*
Transferred from Cutting Department during November	624,995
Direct materials added during November	136,720
Conversion costs added during November	344,685

*The October 30 balance in WIP – Molding Department ($54,000) consist of the following amounts: transferred in costs, $30,405; direct materials costs, $6,680; and conversion costs, $16,915. Complete the following Production Cost Report.

Production Cost Report
Molding Department
November 2003

Unit Reconciliation

Units in Beginning WIP	5,000
Units started during November	45,000
Units to account for	50,000
Units completed and transferred	38,000
Units in Ending WIP (80% materials, 60% Conversion)	12,000
Units accounted for	50,000

Cost per Equivalent Unit Calculation

	Material	Conversion	Trans.-In	Total
Cost				
Beginning WIP	$ 6,680	$ 16,915	$ 30,405	$ 54,000
Cost incurred – Nov	136,120	344,685	624,995	1,106,800
Total	$142,800	$361,600	$655,400	$1,160,800
Units				
Units completed	38,000	38,000	38,000	
EU End WIP	9,600	7,200	7,200	
Total	47,600	45,200	45,200	
Cost per EU	$3.00	$8.00	$14.50	$25.50

CHAPTER 4

COST-VOLUME-PROFIT ANALYSIS

CHAPTER INTRODUCTION

The analysis of how costs and profit change when volume changes is referred to as **cost-volume-profit (C-V-P) analysis**. In this chapter, tools are developed to enable managers to answer questions relating to planning, control, and decision making.

Objectives, Terms, and Discussions

LO1   *Identify common cost behavior patterns.*

To perform cost-volume-profit analysis, you need to know how costs behave when business activity (e.g., production volume or sales volume) changes. This section describes some common patterns of cost behavior.

   Variable costs are costs that change in response to changes in volume or activity. Examples of variable costs are direct material, direct labor, indirect material, and sales commissions. Variable costs are typically assumed to change in proportion to changes in activity. For example, if production volume increases by 10 percent, direct materials are expected to increase in total by 10 percent. The variable cost *per unit* does not change when volume or activity changes. Exactly how activity should be measured in analyzing a variable cost depends on the situation. For example, a caterer's food cost (direct material) varies with number of guests served while a boat manufacturer's direct material cost varies with the number of boats produced.

   Fixed costs are costs that do not change in response to changes in activity levels. Examples of fixed costs are depreciation, supervisory salaries, building maintenance, and rent. For example, if fixed costs total $50,000 for the period, whatever the number of units produced, the amount of fixed costs remains at $50,000. However, the amount of fixed cost per unit does change with the level of activity. For example, if 1,000 units are produced, fixed cost per unit is $50 ($50,000/1000 units), but if production increases to 2,000 units, fixed cost per unit decreases to $25 ($25,000/2,000 units).

Mixed costs (also referred to as **semivariable costs**) are costs that contain both a variable cost element and a fixed cost element. For example, if a company leases software for $10,000 per year (fixed cost) plus a charge of $1.00 per hour for use (variable cost), the company's total software cost is a mixed cost. Total production cost is also a mixed cost since it contains material, labor, and both variable and fixed overhead costs.

LO2   *Estimate the relation between cost and activity using account analysis, the high-low method, and scattergraphs.*

To predict how much cost will be incurred at various levels of activity, how much of the total cost is fixed and how much is variable must be determined. Frequently cost information is not broken out in terms of fixed and variable cost. Therefore, the amount of fixed and variable cost must be estimated. In this chapter, four techniques are presented for estimating the amount of fixed and variable cost: account analysis, the scattergraph approach, the high-low method, and regression analysis.

Account analysis is the most common approach to estimating fixed and variable costs. This method requires that the manager use professional judgement to classify costs as either fixed or variable. The total of the costs classified as variable can be divided by a measure of activity to calculate the variable cost per unit of activity. The total of the costs classified as fixed provides the estimate of fixed cost. The account analysis approach is subjective in that different managers using the same set of facts may reach different conclusions regarding the classification of costs into fixed and variable components. Illustrations 4-4 and 4-5 in the text provide examples of estimating fixed and variable costs using account analysis.

Another approach to estimating fixed and variable costs is the scattergraph approach. A manager can gain insight into the relationship between production cost and activity by plotting costs and activity levels. The plot of the data is referred to as a **scattergraph**. Generally, scattergraphs are prepared with cost measured on the vertical axis and activity level measured on the horizontal axis. The preparation of scattergraphs is a simple procedure using the graphical features in spreadsheet programs. To make predictions, managers visually fit a line to the data points with the general idea to try to minimize the deviations of the data points from the fitted line. Illustrations 4-6 and 4-7 in the text give an example of estimating fixed and variable cost using the scattergraph approach.

The **high-low method** fits a straight line to the data points representing the highest and lowest levels of activity. The slope of the line is the estimate of variable cost (because the slope measures the change in cost per unit change in activity), and the intercept (where the line meets the cost axis) is the estimate of total fixed cost. The slope is equal to the change in cost divided by change in activity. Thus the estimate of variable cost (the slope) is calculated as:

$$\text{Estimate of Variable Cost} = \frac{\text{Change in cost}}{\text{Change in activity}}$$

$$\text{Estimate of variable cost} = \frac{\text{Cost at highest level of activity} - \text{Cost at lowest level of activity}}{\text{Highest level of activity} - \text{Lowest level of activity}}$$

The fixed cost equals the difference between total cost and estimated total variable cost. Fixed costs will be the same whether calculated using the highest level of activity or the lowest level of activity. The high-low method is simple to do, but not reliable. Because only the highest and lowest measures of activity are used, these may not be representative of the typical cost behavior.

Regression analysis is a statistical technique that uses all the available data points to estimate the intercept and slope of a cost equation. The line fitted to the data by regression is the best straight-line fit to the data. The formulas used in conducting regression analysis are complex.

However, software programs that perform regression analysis are widely available. Regression analysis is covered in introductory statistics classes and cost accounting classes.

Estimates of fixed and variable costs are only valid for a limited range of activity. The **relevant range** is the range of activity for which estimates and predictions are likely to be accurate. Outside the relevant range, estimates of fixed and variable costs may not be very useful.

LO3   *Perform cost-volume-profit analysis for single products.*

Once fixed and variable costs have been estimated, cost-volume-profit (C-V-P) analysis can be conducted. C-V-P analysis is any analysis that explores the relations among cost, volume or activity levels, and profit. In C-V-P analysis, we make use of the **profit equation** which states that profit is equal to revenue (selling price × quantity) minus variable cost (variable cost per unit × quantity) minus total fixed cost.

$$\text{Profit} = SP(x) - VC(x) - TFC$$

Where x = Quantity of units produced and sold
SP = Selling price per unit
VC = Variable cost per unit
TFC = Total fixed cost

One of the primary uses of C-V-P analysis is to calculate the **break-even point.** The break-even point is the number of units that must be sold for a company to break even—to neither earn a profit nor incur a loss.

To calculate the break-even point, we set the profit equation equal to zero. Then we insert the appropriate selling price, variable cost, and fixed cost information and solve the equation. For example, suppose a product sells for $100 per unit, variable cost are estimated to be $90 per unit, and total fixed costs are estimated to be $80,000. As shown below, a company must sell 8,000 units to break even in a given period.

$$0 = \$100(x) - \$90(x) - \$80,000$$
$$0 = \$10(x) - \$80,000$$
$$\$10x = \$80,000$$
$$x = 8,000 \text{ units}$$

To express how close managers expect to be to the break-even level, they may calculate the margin of safety. The **margin of safety** is the difference between the expected level of sales and break-even sales.

The profit equation can be rewritten by combining the terms with x in them to yield the **contribution margin.** The contribution margin is defined as the difference between the selling price per unit (SP) and variable cost per unit (VC). Profit is then calculated as the difference between the contribution margin times the level of activity and the total fixed costs (TFC).

$$\text{Profit} = SP(x) - VC(x) - TFC$$
$$\text{Profit} = (SP\text{-}VC)(x) - TFC$$
$$\text{Profit} = \text{Contribution margin}(x) - TFC$$

The contribution margin measures the amount each unit sold contributes to covering fixed cost and increasing profit. When sales and production increase by one unit, the company benefits from revenue (selling price), but that benefit is reduced by variable cost per unit. Fixed costs do not affect the *incremental* profit associated with selling an additional unit because fixed costs are not affected by changes in volume. If we solve the profit equation for the sales quantity in units (x), we get the following expression.

$$x = \frac{\text{Profit} + \text{TFC}}{\text{SP} - \text{VC}} \qquad \text{or} \qquad x = \frac{\text{Profit} + \text{TFC}}{\text{Contribution Margin}}$$

The **contribution margin ratio** provides a measure of the contribution of every sales dollar to covering fixed cost and generating a profit. It is equal to the contribution margin per unit divided by the selling price.

$$\text{Contribution margin ratio} = \frac{\text{SP} - \text{VC}}{\text{SP}}$$

We can express the profit equation in terms of the contribution margin ratio as:

$$\text{Sales (in dollars)} = \frac{\text{Profit} + \text{TFC}}{\text{Contribution margin ratio}}$$

The profit equation also can show how profit will be affected by various options under consideration by management. Such analysis is sometimes referred to as **"what if" analysis** because it examines *what* will happen *if* a particular action is taken.

LO4 *Perform cost-volume-profit analysis for multiple products.*

C-V-P analysis can be extended to cover multiple products. If the products a company sells are similar, the weighted average contribution margin per unit can be used in C-V-P analysis. The weighted average contribution margin per unit is calculated exactly the same as contribution margin per unit for a single product except that overall figures are used. If the products that a company sells are substantially different, C-V-P analysis should be performed using the contribution margin ratio. When a company sells many different products, how many *units* must be sold to break even or make a profit is not appropriate. A more appropriate measure is how much *sales* must be made to break even or generate a profit. To calculate how much sales dollars are needed, the contribution margin ratio, rather than the contribution margin per unit, should be used. The contribution margin ratio can also be used to analyze the effect on net income of a change in total company sales.

Whenever C-V-P analysis is performed, a number of assumptions are made that affect the validity of the analysis:
- Costs can be accurately separated into their fixed and variable components
- Fixed costs remain fixed
- Variable costs per unit do not change over the activity levels of interest

LO5 *Discuss the effect of operating leverage.*

Operating leverage relates to the level of fixed versus variable costs in a firm's cost structure. Firms that have relatively high levels of fixed cost are said to have high operating leverage. The level of operating leverage is important because it affects the change in profit when sales change. Firms that have high operating leverages are generally thought to be more risky because they tend to have large fluctuations in profit when sales fluctuate.

Because of fixed costs in the cost structure, when sales increase by 10 percent, profit will increase by more than 10 percent. The only time that profit will increase by the same percent as sales in when all costs are variable.

LO6   *Use the contribution margin per unit of the constraint to analyze situations involving a resource constraint.*

In many cases there are constraints on how many items can be produced or how much service can be provided. Examples of constraints faced by managers include shortages of space, equipment, and labor. In such cases, the focus shifts from the contribution margin per unit to the contribution margin per unit of the constraint.

LOA1   *Calculate income using variable costing.*

Most income statements prepared for external purposes use **full costing** (also called **absorption costing**). In full costing, inventory costs include direct material, direct labor, and all manufacturing overhead. Because manufacturing overhead includes both variable and fixed cost elements, fixed and variable costs are commingled and it is difficult to perform "what if" analysis.

An alternative to full costing is variable costing. In **variable costing**, only variable production costs are included in product costs. All fixed production costs are treated as period costs and are expensed in the period incurred.

The only difference in full costing and variable costing is the treatment of fixed manufacturing overhead. Under full costing, fixed manufacturing overhead is included in inventory (Work-in-Process or Finished Goods) and enter into the determination of expense only when the inventory is sold (Cost of Goods Sold). Under variable costing, fixed manufacturing overhead enters into the determination of expense in the same way as other, nonmanufacturing, period costs.

An income statement prepared using variable costing classifies all expenses in terms of their cost behavior—either fixed or variable. With variable and fixed costs separated, the contribution margin can be easily calculated. If the quantity produced exceeds the quantity sold during the period, full costing yields a higher income than variable costing. However, if the quantity sold exceeds the quantity produced during a period, variable costing yields a higher income than full costing. This happens because, under full costing, the units sold out of beginning inventory include fixed overhead of a prior period. If the quantity sold is equal to the quantity produced during the period, both methods result in the same level of income.

Review of Key Terms

Absorption costing: An approach to product costing that includes direct material, direct labor, and both fixed and variable manufacturing overhead in product cost. Also referred to as full costing. The alternative to absorption costing is variable costing, which includes direct material, direct labor, and variable (but not fixed) manufacturing overhead.

Account analysis: A method of estimating cost behavior which requires professional judgment to classify costs as either fixed or variable. The total of the costs classified as variable are divided by a measure of activity to calculate the variable cost per unit of activity. The total of the costs classified as fixed provides the estimate of fixed cost.

Break-even point: The number of units a company must sell to earn a zero profit.

Contribution margin: The difference between sales and variable costs.

Contribution margin ratio: The contribution margin divided by sales or the contribution margin per unit divided by the selling price.

Fixed cost: Costs that do not change when there is a change in business activity.

Full costing: An approach to product costing that includes direct material, direct labor, and both fixed and variable manufacturing overhead in product cost. Also referred to as absorption costing. The alternative to full costing is variable costing which includes direct material, direct labor, and variable (but not fixed) manufacturing overhead.

High-low method: A method of estimating fixed and variable cost components in which a straight line is fitted to the data points representing the highest and lowest levels of activity.

Margin of safety: The difference between the expected level of sales and break-even sales.

Mixed cost: Costs that contain both variable and fixed cost elements.

Operating leverage: Level of fixed versus variable costs in a firm's cost structure. Firms that have relatively high levels of fixed cost are said to have high operating leverage.

Profit equation: Equation that states that profit is equal to revenue (selling price times quantity) minus variable cost (variable cost per unit times quantity) minus total fixed cost.

Regression analysis: A statistical technique used to estimate the intercept (an estimate of fixed cost) and the slope (an estimate of variable cost) of a cost equation.

Relevant range: The range of activity for which estimates and predictions are likely to be accurate.

Scattergraph: A graph of costs at various activity levels.

Variable cost: Those costs that increase or decrease in response to increases or decreases in business activity.

Variable costing: An alternative to full costing in which only variable production costs are included in inventory—fixed production costs are treated as period costs.

"What if" analysis: An examination of the results of various courses of action.

Chapter 4 – True/False

_____T_____ 1. Two common variable costs are direct material and direct labor.

_____F_____ 2. Variable costs change inversely with changes in activity.

_____F_____ 3. Mixed costs contain elements of both direct material and direct labor.

_____F_____ 4. The account analysis method is an objective approach in that it does not require managers to use professional judgement to classify costs as fixed or variable costs.

_____T_____ 5. Using the high-low method to classify costs as fixed or variable, the slope of the line is the estimate of variable cost.

_____F_____ 6. Basically, C-V-P analysis explores the relations among costs, volume, and performance.

_____F_____ 7. To calculate the break-even point, the profit equation is set to $1, and then the appropriate selling price, variable cost, and fixed cost information are inserted into the equation.

_____F_____ 8. The contribution margin ratio is equal to the contribution margin per unit divided by the variable cost.

_____T_____ 9. Firms that have relatively high levels of fixed cost are said to have high operating leverage.

_____F_____ 10. The only time that you expect profit to increase by the same percent as sales is when all costs are fixed.

_____T_____ 11. In full costing, inventory costs include direct material, direct labor, and all manufacturing overhead.

_____T_____ 12. In variable costing, variable production costs are included in product costs while fixed production costs are treated as period costs.

Chapter 4 – Key Terms Matching

Match the terms found in Chapter 4 with the following definitions:

a. absorption costing
b. break-even point
c. contribution margin
d. high-low method
e. mixed cost
f. margin of safety

g. operating leverage
h. profit equation
i. regression analysis
j. scattergraph
k. variable costing
l. "what if" analysis

_____J_____ 1. A graph of costs at various activity levels.

_____h_____ 2. Equation that states that profit is equal to revenue (selling price times quantity) minus variable cost (variable cost per unit times quantity) minus total fixed cost.

_____L_____ 3. An examination of the results of various courses of action.

_____B_____ 4. The number of units a company must sell to earn a zero profit.

_____E_____ 5. Costs that contain both variable and fixed elements.

_____A_____ 6. An approach to product costing that includes direct material, direct labor, and both fixed and variable manufacturing overhead in product cost. Also referred to as full costing.

_____C_____ 7. The difference between sales and variable costs.

_____i_____ 8. A statistical technique used to estimate the intercept (an estimate of fixed cost) and the slope (an estimate of variable cost) of a cost equation.

_____F_____ 9. The difference between the expected level of sales and break-even sales.

_____k_____ 10. An alternative to full costing in which only variable production costs are included in inventory—fixed production costs are treated as period costs.

_____G_____ 11. Level of fixed versus variable costs in a firm's cost structure.

_____D_____ 12. A method of estimating fixed and variable cost components in which a straight line is fitted to the data points representing the highest and lowest levels of activity.

Chapter 4 – Multiple Choice

1. Mixed costs are also referred to as:
    a. double costs.
    b. assorted costs.
    c. sundry costs.
    d. semivariable costs.

2. Which of the following methods is the most common approach to estimating fixed and variable costs?
    a. Scattergraph
    b. Regression analysis
    c. Account analysis
    d. High-low method

3. Each point on the scattergraph represents one pair of:
    a. cost and activity values.
    b. variable cost and revenue values.
    c. fixed cost and revenue values.
    d. revenue and activity values.

Michael Company produces lawn mowers. The selling price per mower is $750. The variable cost per mower is $400 and the fixed cost per period is $7,700. Michael Company expects to sell 25 lawn mowers during the period. Use the information to answer questions 4 through 7.

4. The contribution margin per unit is:
    a. $400.
    b. $350.
    c. $150.
    d. none of the above.

5. The break-even point in units is:
    a. 25.
    b. 24.
    c. 38.
    d. 22.

6. The break-even point in dollars is:
    a. $17,700.
    b. $16,500.
    c. $18,750.
    d. none of the above.

7. The contribution margin ratio is:
    a. 53.3%.
    b. 46.7%.
    c. 88%.
    d. none of the above.

8.   The margin of safety is:
   a. $750.
   b. $350.
   c. $2,250.
   d. $1,100.

9.   The three elements of the profit equation are:
   a. selling price per unit, variable cost per unit, and fixed cost per unit.
   b. total revenue, total variable costs, and total fixed cost.
   c. selling price per unit, variable cost per unit, and total fixed costs.
   d. selling price per unit, total variable costs, and fixed cost per unit.

10.   The contribution margin ratio provides a measure of:
   a. the contribution of every sales dollar to covering fixed cost and generating a profit.
   b. the contribution of every sales dollar to covering variable cost and generating a profit.
   c. the contribution of every sales dollar to covering variable and fixed costs and generating a profit.
   d. none of the above.

11.   Which of the following assumptions made when using C-V-P analysis might affect the validity of the analysis?
   a. Costs can be accurately separated into their fixed and variable components.
   b. Fixed costs remain fixed and variable costs per unit do not change over the activity levels of interest.
   c. Both a and b
   d. Neither a nor b

12.   In full costing, inventory costs include:
   a. direct material, direct labor, variable overhead, and fixed overhead.
   b. direct material, direct labor, and variable overhead.
   c. direct material, direct labor, and fixed overhead.
   d. none of the above.

$$10 — 10?$$
$$y — 30$$

$$x = \frac{10 \times 30}{100}$$

Exercise 4 – 1   During a recent six-month period, Pam's Laundry had the following monthly volume of laundry and total monthly utilities expense:

	Pounds of Laundry	Utilities Expense
July	19,750	$1,298
August	14,000	1,110
September	28,800	1,760
October	26,500	1,680
November	34,000	2,070
December	24,000	1,580

Required:

1.   Compute the variable cost per pound of laundry.

	Pounds of Laundry	Utilities Expense
High level of activity	34,000	2,070
Low level of activity	14,000	1,110
Change	20,000	960

$$\frac{\Delta \text{Cost}}{\Delta \text{ACT}}$$

$$\frac{\text{Estimate of}}{\text{Variable cost}} = \frac{\text{Change in cost}}{\text{Change in activity}} \quad \frac{\$ \ 960}{20,000 \ \text{pounds}} = \$ \ 0.048 / \text{unit}$$

2.   Compute the total fixed cost per month.

Total cost at the high level of activity   2,070

Less variable cost   1,632

Fixed cost   438

3.   Compute the total amount of utilities expense that would be incurred at a level of 32,000 pounds of laundry.

Variable cost at a level of 32,000 pounds   1,536

Fixed cost at a level of 32,000 pounds   438

Total utility cost at a level of 32,000 pounds   1,974

Exercise 4 – 2 Woody's Company charges a service fee of $600 per unit. Variable costs per unit are $450 and fixed costs total $150,000

1.   What is the contribution margin per unit?

$SP = \$600/unit$
$VC = \$450/unit$
$FC = \$150,000$

$CM = SP-VC = \underline{\$150/unit}$

2.   What is the contribution margin ratio?

$CMR = \dfrac{SP-VC}{SP} = \boxed{25\%}$

3.   Compute the break-even point in units.

$X = \dfrac{FC}{SP-VC} = \dfrac{FC}{CM} = \dfrac{150K}{150} = \boxed{1,000 \ UNITS}$

4.   Compute the break-even point in dollar volume of revenue.

$BEP(\$) = \underline{\$600,000}$

5.   Prove your answers in parts 3 and 4 by preparing a contribution income statement in good order.

Woody's Company
Contribution Income Statement
June 30, 2004

Revenue	$\underline{600,000}$
Less variable costs	$\underline{450,000}$
Contribution margin	$\underline{150,000}$
Less fixed costs	$\underline{150,000}$
Net income	$\underline{\underline{0}}$

Exercise 4-3 For several years, Bellagio's Restaurant has offered a lunch special for $7.00. Monthly fixed expenses have been $4,200. The variable cost of a meal has been $2.10. Anthony Bellagio, the owner, believes that by remodeling the restaurant and upgrading the food services, he can increase the price of the lunch special to $7.40. Monthly fixed expenses would increase to $4,800 and the variable expenses would increase to $2.96 per meal.

1.   Compute Bellagio's monthly break-even sales in dollars before remodeling.

$SP = \$7 /unit$

$FC = \$4,200$

$VC = \$2.10$

$BEP = \dfrac{TFC}{SP-VC} = \dfrac{4,200}{7-2.10} = 857.14$

$BE \text{ sales } \$ = 857.14 \times 7 = \boxed{\$6,000.0}$

2.   Compute Bellagio's monthly break-even sales in dollars after remodeling.

$SP = \$7.40$

$FC = \$4,800$

$VC = \$2.96$

$BEP = \dfrac{TFC}{SP-VC} = \dfrac{4,800}{7.40-2.96} = 1,081.08 \times 7.40 = $

$8,000$

3.   What recommendation would you make to Anthony Bellagio concerning remodeling the restaurant?

By remodeling, Bellagios will increase its operating leverage, therefore increasing its risk. It would take more sales to break-even. Bellagio's should not renovate

Problem 4 – 4 The Tucker Company manufactures and sells a single product. The company's sales and expenses for the most recent month are given below:

	Total	Per Unit $	%
Sales	$450,000	$20	100
Less variable expenses	315,000	14	70
Contribution margin	$135,000	$6	30
Less fixed expenses	75,000		
Net income	$60,000		

1.   What is the monthly break-even point in units and in sales dollars?

$$BEP = 75,000/(20-14) \{ 12,500.00 \text{ units} \times 20 = \$250,000$$

2.   Without resorting to computations, what is the total contribution margin at the break-even point?

$$250,000 \times 30\% = \$75,000$$

3.   How many units would have to be sold each month to earn a minimum target net income of $18,000?   Prove your answer by preparing a contribution income statement at the target level of sales.

$$P = SPx - VCx - TFC \quad \Rightarrow \quad x = \frac{P + TFC}{CM} = \frac{18,000 + 75,000}{(20-14)} \{ 15,500 \text{ units}$$

Sales	310,000
VC	217,000
CM	93,000
FC	75,000
NI	18,000

4.   Compute Tucker's degree of operating leverage using the original data.

$$\frac{CM}{P} = OL \qquad \frac{135,000}{60,000} = 2.25$$

5.   Assuming Tucker increases sales by 10%, how much will net income increase?

$$OL = 2.25 \quad | \quad \text{sales increase } 10\% \to$$
$$NI = 2.25 \times 10\% = 22.5\%$$

6.   Prove your answer in part 5 by preparing a contribution income statement at that level of activity.

$$\frac{SP_x - VC_x}{SP_x - VC_x - FC} = OL \qquad \frac{x(SP-VC)}{x(SP-VC)-FC} = OL$$

Problem 4 – 5
Pedals R Us is a small manufacturer of mountain bicycles. The bikes sell for $500 each. The variable costs of each unit includes the following:

Direct materials	$130
Direct labor	150
Manufacturing overhead	60

In addition, $450,000 of fixed overhead is incurred in each period. Selling and administrative costs are fixed costs that total $135,000 and $225,000 respectively.

On January 1, 2003, there was no beginning inventory of finished goods. During the year 15,000 bikes were produced. At the end of the year there were 5,000 bikes in ending inventory.

1. Assuming Pedals Are Us uses absorption costing, what is the unit cost for one bicycle?

2. Assuming Pedals Are Us uses variable costing, what is the unit cost for one bicycle?

3. Prepare an income statement for Pedals Are Us using absorption costing.

4. Prepare an income statement for Pedals Are Us using variable costing.

Solutions – Chapter 4 – True/False

1.   T
2.   F   Variable costs change proportionately with changes in activity.
3.   F   Mixed costs contain elements of both fixed cost and variable cost.
4.   F   The account analysis method is a subjective approach that requires managers to use professional judgement to classify costs as fixed or variable costs.
5.   T
6.   F   Basically, C-V-P analysis explores the relations among costs, volume, and profit.
7.   F   To calculate the break-even point, the profit equation is set to zero, and then insert the appropriate selling price, variable cost, and fixed cost information.
8.   F   The contribution margin ratio is equal to the contribution margin per unit divided by the selling price.
9.   T
10.   F   The only time that you expect profit to increase by the same percent as sales is when all costs are variable.
11.   T
12.   T

Solutions – Key Terms Matching

1.   j. scattergraph
2.   h. profit equation
3.   l. "what if" analysis
4.   b. break-even point
5.   e. mixed cost
6.   a. absorption costing
7.   c. contribution margin
8.   i. regression analysis
9.   f margin of safety
10.   k. variable costing
11.   g. operating leverage
12.   d. high-low method

Solutions – Multiple Choice

1.   d
2.   c
3.   a
4.   b
5.   d
6.   b
7.   b
8.   c
9.   c
10.   a
11.   c
12.   a

Solution – Exercise 4 – 1
During a recent six-month period, Pam's Laundry had the following monthly volume of laundry and total monthly utilities expense:

	Pounds of Laundry	**Utilities Expense**
July	19,750	$1,298
August	14,000	1,110
September	28,800	1,760
October	26,500	1,680
November	34,000	2,070
December	24,000	1,580

Required:

1.   Compute the variable cost per pound of laundry.

	Pounds of Laundry	Utilities Expense
High level of activity	34,000	$2,070
Low level of activity	14,000	1,110
Change	2,000	$ 960

$$\text{Estimate of Variable cost} = \frac{\text{Change in cost}}{\text{Change in activity}} \quad \frac{\$960}{20,000 \text{ pounds}} = \$.048$$

2.   Compute the total fixed cost per month.

Total cost at the high level of activity	$2,070
Less variable cost (34,000 lbs. × $.048)	1,632
Fixed cost	$ 438

3.   Compute the total amount of utilities expense that would be incurred at a level of 32,000 pounds of laundry.

Variable cost at 32,000 pounds (32,000 × $.048)	$1,536
Fixed cost at a level of 32,000 pounds	438
Total utility cost at a level of 32,000 pounds	$1,974

Solution – Exercise 4 – 2 Woody's Company charges a service fee of $600 per unit. Variable costs per unit are $450 and fixed costs total $150,000.

1. What is the contribution margin per unit?

Revenue	$600
Variable cost	450
Contribution margin	$150

2. What is the contribution margin ratio?

Revenue	$600	100%
Variable costs	450	75%
Contribution margin	$150	25%

3. Compute the break-even point in units.

$150,000 ÷ $150 = 1,000 units

4. Compute the break-even point in dollar volume of revenue.

$150,000 ÷ .25 = $600,000

5. Prove your answers in parts 3 and 4 by preparing a contribution income statement in good order.

Woody's Company
Contribution Income Statement
June 30, 2004

Revenue (1,000 units @ $600)	$600,000
Less variable costs (1,000 units @ $450)	450,000
Contribution margin	$150,000
Less fixed costs	150,000
Net income	- 0 -

Solution – Exercise 4-3
For several years, Bellagio's Restaurant has offered a lunch special for $7.00. Monthly fixed expenses have been 4,200. The variable cost of a meal has been $4.20. Anthony Bellagio, the owner, believes that by remodeling the restaurant and upgrading the food services, he can increase the price of the lunch special to $7.50. Monthly fixed expenses would increase to $4,800 and the variable expenses would increase to $4.50 per meal.

1. Compute Bellagio's monthly break-even sales in dollars before remodeling.

Sales	$7.00	100%	Fixed costs ÷ CM ratio = BEP in $ volume
Variable costs	2.10	30%	
Contribution margin	$4.90	70%	$4,200 ÷ .70 = $6000

2. Compute Bellagio's monthly break-even sales in dollars after remodeling.

Sales	$7.40	100%
Variable costs	2.96	40%
Contribution margin	$4.44	60%

Fixed costs ÷ CM ratio = BEP in $ volume
$4,800   ÷   .60   = $8,000

3. What recommendation would you make to Anthony Bellagio concerning remodeling the restaurant?

As an accounting student, I would recommend that you not remodel the restaurant building. At the present time, you need to have monthly revenue of only $6,000 to break even. However, with the remodeling, you would need monthly revenues of $8,000 to break-even.

Solution – Problem 4 – 4 The Tucker Company manufactures and sells a single product. The company's sales and expenses for the most recent month are given below:

	Total	Per Unit	
Sales	$450,000	$20	100%
Less variable expenses	315,000	14	70%
Contribution margin	$135,000	$ 6	30%
Less fixed expenses	75,000		
Net income	$ 60,000		

1. What is the monthly break-even point in units and in sales dollars?

Fixed costs ÷ CM per unit = BEP in units $75,000 ÷ $6 = 12,500 units

Fixed costs ÷ CM ratio = BEP in $ volume $75,000 ÷ .30 = $250,000

2. Without resorting to computations, what is the total contribution margin at the break-even point?

$75,000 – At the break-even point, contribution margin is always equal to fixed expenses.

3. How many units would have to be sold each month to earn a minimum target net income of $18,000? Prove your answer by preparing a contribution income statement at the target level of sales.

(Fixed cost + Target profit) ÷ CM per unit = Units to earn target profit

($75,000 + $18,000) ÷ $6 = 15,500 units

Sales (15,500 @ $20)	$310,000
Variable costs (15,500 @ $14)	217,000
Contribution margin	$ 93,000
Fixed cost	75,000
Net income	$ 18,000

4. Compute Tucker's degree of operating leverage using the original data.

Contribution margin ÷ Net income = Operating leverage

$135,000 ÷ $60,000 = 2.25

5. Assuming Tucker increases sales by 10%, how much will net income increase?

Increase in sales multiplied by operating leverage = increase in net income.

10% × 2.25 = .225 or 22.5 %

Solution – Problem 4 – 4 (continued)

6.   Prove your answer in part 5 by preparing a contribution income statement at that level of activity.

Sales	$495,000
Less variable expenses	346,500
Contribution margin	$148,500
Less fixed expenses	75,000
Net income	$ 73,500

$73,500 - $60,000 = $13,500 ÷ $60,000 = .225 or 22.5%

Solution – Problem 4 – 5   Pedals R Us is a small manufacturer of mountain bicycles. The bikes sell for $500 each. The variable costs of each unit includes the following:

Direct materials	$130
Direct labor	150
Manufacturing overhead	60

In addition, $450,000 of fixed overhead is incurred in each period. Selling and administrative costs are fixed costs that total $135,000 and $225,000 respectively.

On January 1, 2003, there was no beginning inventory of finished goods. During the year 15,000 bikes were produced. At the end of the year there were 5,000 bikes in ending inventory.

1.   Assuming Pedals Are Us uses absorption costing, what is the unit cost for one bicycle?

Direct materials	$130
Direct labor	150
Variable manufacturing overhead	60
Fixed manufacturing overhead ($450,000 ÷ 15,000)	30
Total	$370

2.   Assuming Pedals Are Us uses variable costing, what is the unit cost for one bicycle?

Direct materials	$130
Direct labor	150
Variable manufacturing overhead	60
Total	$340

Solution – Problem 4 – 5 (continued)

3. Prepare an income statement for Pedals Are Us using absorption costing.

Sales		$5,000,000
Cost of goods sold		
Beginning inventory	- 0 -	
Cost of goods manufactured	$5,550,000	
Less ending inventory	1,850,000	3,700,000
Gross margin		$1,300,000
Less operating expenses		
Selling expenses	$ 135,000	
Administrative expenses	225,000	360,000
Net income		$ 940,000

4. Prepare an income statement for Pedals Are Us using variable costing.

Sales		$5,000,000
Less: Variable costs		
Variable cost of goods sold (10,000 @ $340)		3,400,000
Contribution margin		1,600,000
Less: Fixed costs		
Fixed manufacturing overhead	$450,000	
Selling expenses	135,000	
Administrative expenses	225,000	810,000
Net income		$790,000

CHAPTER **5**

COST ALLOCATION AND ACTIVITY-BASED COSTING

CHAPTER INTRODUCTION

Companies that produce more than one product or provide more than one type of service invariably have indirect costs because resources are shared by the products or services. Various departments may also have common or shared resources. For example, all services provided may use the same computer facility or several products may be manufactured using the same piece of equipment. Because indirect costs associated with shared resources cannot be directly traced to products or services, some means of assigning them must be developed. The process of assigning indirect costs is referred to as **cost allocation**.

Objectives, Terms, and Discussions

LO1 *Explain why indirect costs are allocated.*

Companies allocate cost to products, services, and departments for four major reasons:
- To provide information needed to make appropriate decisions
- To reduce the frivolous use of common resources
- To encourage managers to evaluate the efficiency of internally provided services
- To calculate the "full cost" of products for financial reporting purposes and for determining cost-based prices

When managers use a company resource and receive an allocation of its cost they are, in essence, receiving a charge for its use. The more a manager uses the company resource, the more cost he or she will receive, thus reducing profit for his or her operation or department. From a decision-making standpoint, the allocated cost should measure the opportunity cost of using a company resource. In practice, however, this is difficult to operationalize because the opportunity cost may quickly change. The opportunity cost idea is still a useful benchmark and managers should ask themselves how close is the allocation to the opportunity cost of use—the closer, the better.

Some managers would argue that because some common resources are fixed costs (e.g., costs associated with running a computer), divisions should not be charged for using the service or facility, since use creates no incremental cost. However, if divisions do not incur any charge for using the service or facility, they may tend to use the resource for frivolous or nonessential purposes. Frivolous use may have some hidden costs such as slower service to departments that need to use the resource while it is being used unnecessarily by another department. One way to eliminate frivolous use is to charge for the use of centrally provided services. A common way to charge for use is to allocate the cost.

Cost allocation is also useful because it encourages managers to evaluate the services for which they are being charged. If services are free, such as janitorial or computer services, then users do not have an incentive to evaluate these services carefully. If the users receive an allocation of the cost of the services, the users have a strong incentive to look critically at the services and consider the possibility of lower-cost alternatives.

GAAP requires full costing for external reporting purposes. Indirect production costs must be allocated to goods produced to meet this requirement. Full cost information is also required when a company has an agreement whereby the amount of revenue depends on the amount of cost incurred (cost-plus contracts). A problem with cost-plus contracts is that they create an incentive to unjustly allocate as much cost as possible to those projects.

LO2 *Describe the cost allocation process.*

The first step in the cost allocation process is to determine the product, service, or department that is to receive the allocation. The object of the allocation is referred to as **the cost objective**. For example, if computer-processing costs are allocated to contracts worked on by a computer-aided design group, the contracts are the cost objectives.

The second step in the cost allocation process is to form **cost pools**. A cost pool is a grouping of individual costs whose total is allocated using one allocation base. For example, all of the costs in the maintenance department could be treated as a cost pool. The cost pool would include the wages of maintenance workers, supplies, small tools, and other maintenance department cost items. The overriding concern in forming a cost pool is to ensure that the costs in the pool are homogeneous or similar. One way to evaluate the homogeneity of costs is to compare the allocations with the allocations that result from breaking the pool up into smaller pools and using a variety of allocation bases. If there is not a considerable difference in the allocations, then the costs in the pool are considered to be homogeneous.

The third step in the allocation process is to select an allocation base that relates the cost pool to the cost objectives. The allocation base must be some characteristic that is common to all of the cost objectives. Direct labor hours, direct labor cost, machine hours, sales dollars, total assets, and divisional profit are examples of characteristics that could be used as allocation bases. The allocation should be based on a **cause-and-effect relationship**. That is, the allocation base selected should relate costs to cost objectives that caused the cost to be incurred.

When indirect costs are fixed, establishing cause-and-effect relationships may not be feasible. Therefore, accountants use other criteria such as relative benefits, ability to bear cost, and equity to determine amounts to be allocated to various users. The **relative benefits** concept suggests that the allocation base should result in more costs being allocated to the cost objectives that benefit most from incurring the cost. The **ability to bear costs** idea suggests that the allocation base should result in more cost being allocated to products, services, or departments that are more profitable. The **equity** notion suggests that the allocation base should result in allocations that are perceived to be fair or equitable. Equity may be difficult to apply since different managers will have different perceptions of what is an equitable allocation.

LO3   *Discuss allocation of service department costs.*

The organizational units in most manufacturing firms can be classified as either production departments or service departments. Production departments engage in direct manufacturing activity, whereas service departments provide indirect support. For example, assembly and finishing departments are production departments, while maintenance and personnel departments are service departments.

One method of allocating service department costs is called the **direct method**. Using the direct method, service department costs are allocated to production departments, but not to other service departments. For example, if the personnel department (a service department) has budgeted costs of $20,000 and the department's services are used by Department A and Department B, production departments, and maintenance, a service department, then the $20,000 will be allocated only to Departments A and B. If Department A employs 25 workers, Department B employs 75 workers, and maintenance employs 35 workers, the personnel cost can be allocated based on number of employees in each department. Thus Department A will be charged $5,000 (25/100 × $20,000) while Department B will be charged $15,000 (75/100 × $20,000). Remember, since maintenance is a service department, it will not receive any allocated costs of the personnel department. It is generally a good idea to allocate budgeted rather than actual service department costs. Allocating budgeted costs prevents service departments from passing the cost of inefficiencies and waste to other departments.

LO4   *Identify potential problems with cost allocation.*

Problems with cost allocation arise for several reasons:
- Allocations of costs that are not controllable
- Arbitrary allocations
- Allocations of fixed costs that make the fixed costs appear to be variable costs
- Allocations of manufacturing overhead to products using too few overhead cost pools
- Use of only volume-related bases

Performance evaluations of managers and operations are facilitated by a system of accounting that traces revenues and costs to organizational units and individuals with related responsibility for generating revenue and controlling costs. Such a system is referred to as a **responsibility accounting system**. Cost allocation is generally required in a responsibility accounting system because one organizational unit is often responsible for the costs incurred by another organizational unit. Most accountants believe that managers should be held responsible only for cost they can control. These costs, called **controllable costs**, are affected by the manager's decisions. For example, allocating the cost of a building to the performance report of a supervisor responsible for controlling labor cost is not appropriate. If allocated costs beyond a manager's control appear on the manager's performance report, these costs may cause considerable frustration because the performance evaluations should reflect the manager's own strengths and weaknesses.

Allocations of costs are to a great extent inherently arbitrary. In most cost allocation situations, determining the one "correct" or "valid" allocation is not possible. Various allocation bases may be equally justifiable, but may result in substantially different allocations.

One of the most significant problems associated with cost allocation is due to the fact that the allocation process may make fixed costs appear to be variable costs. This happens when fixed costs are **unitized**—that is, stated on a per unit basis. To remedy the problem, allocations of fixed costs should be made in such a way that they appear fixed to the managers whose departments receive the allocations. This is achieved by **lump-sum allocations** of fixed costs. A lump-sum allocation is an allocation of a predetermined amount that is not affected by changes in the activity level of the organizational unit receiving the allocation.

Some companies assign overhead to products using only one or two overhead cost pools. Although the approach has the benefit of being simple and easy to use, product costs may be seriously distorted when only a small number of cost pools are used. In general, product costs will be more accurate when more overhead cost pools are used. Decisions that rely on product cost information, such as product pricing decisions, will also be improved. However, the more pools that are formed, the more costly the recordkeeping becomes.

A final problem is that some manufacturing companies allocate manufacturing overhead to products using only measures of production volume (e.g., direct labor or machine hours) as allocation bases. However, not all overhead costs vary with volume. This problem is solved by using activity-based costing (ABC).

LO5 *Discuss activity-based costing (ABC) and cost drivers.*

ABC costing was introduced in Chapter 2 dealing with job-order costing. Using only measures of production volume as allocation bases to allocate overhead is referred to as the "traditional approach." The problem with the traditional approach is that it assumes that all overhead costs are proportional to production volume. However, many overhead costs (e.g., setting up equipment, inspecting raw materials, or handling material) are not proportional to volume. The result is that high-volume products are often overcosted, and low-volume products are undercosted.

In an ABC approach, companies identify the major activities that cause overhead costs to be incurred. Some of these activities relate to production volume, but others do not. The costs of the resources consumed performing these activities are grouped into cost pools. Illustration 5-8 in the textbook displays common activities and associated cost drivers. The costs are then assigned to products using a measure of activity referred to as a **cost driver**. The steps involved in the ABC approach are:

- Identify major activities
- Group costs of activities into cost pools
- Identify measures of activities—the cost drivers
- Relate costs to products using the cost drivers

One major benefit of using ABC systems is that ABC is less likely than traditional costing systems to undercost complex, low-volume products and overcost simple, high-volume products. A second benefit is that ABC may lead to improvements in cost control. A major disadvantage of ABC is its expense; an ABC system is more costly to develop and maintain than a traditional costing system. Another limitation of ABC is that, in practice, it is used to develop the full cost of products. Because full costs include allocations of costs that are fixed, the cost per unit generated by the ABC system does not measure the incremental costs needed to produce an item. Recall that incremental information is what is needed to make decisions.

LO6 *Discuss activity-based management (ABM).*

Activity-based management (ABM) is a management tool that involves analyzing and costing activities with the goal of improving efficiency and effectiveness. ABM is closely related to ABC, but the two schemes differ in their primary goals. While ABC focuses on activities with the goal of measuring the costs of products and services produced by them, ABM focuses on activities with the goal of managing the activities themselves. For example, consider activities involved in setting up equipment for a production run. ABC seeks to measure the cost of setups and then assign a cost to products based on how many setups each product requires. The goal of ABM is to focus on ways to improve the setup process and ways to eliminate the demand for set-up activity, thereby reducing setup cost.

Remember, you get what you measure. Allocations affect the profit that managers have reported on their performance report. Thus, managers pay attention to controlling the allocation base, since more use of the allocation base results in higher costs and lower profits.

Review of Key Terms

Ability to bear costs approach to allocation: The notion in cost allocation that the allocation base should result in more costs being allocated to products, services, or departments that are more profitable.

Activity-based management: A management approach that involves analyzing and costing activities with the goal of improving efficiency and effectiveness.

Cause-and-effect-relationship: An allocation of cost to the cost objective that caused it to be incurred.

Controllable costs: A cost that a manager can influence by the decisions he or she makes.

Cost allocation: The process of assigning indirect costs.

Cost driver: A measure of the activity, related to a cost pool, that is used to allocate cost.

Cost objective: The object of cost allocation.

Cost pool: A grouping of overhead costs based on the major activity that created them. Also, a grouping of individual costs whose total is allocated using one allocation base.

Direct method of allocation: A method of allocating service department costs to production departments, which does not allow for allocation of costs among service departments.

Equity approach to allocation: An attempt to allocate costs in a way that is fair to interested parties.

Lump-sum allocation: Allocations of fixed costs in which predetermined amounts are allocated regardless of changes in the level of activity.

Relative benefits approach to allocation: The notion in cost allocation that the allocation base should result in more cost being allocated to the cost objectives that benefit most from incurring the cost.

Responsibility accounting system: A system of accounting that traces revenues and costs to organizational units and individuals with related responsibility for generating revenue and controlling costs.

Unitized fixed costs: Fixed costs stated on a per unit basis.

Chapter 5 – True/False

__F__   1. From a decision-making standpoint, the allocated cost should measure the direct cost of using a company resource.

__T__   2. Cost allocation encourages managers to evaluate the services for which they are being charged and eliminates frivolous use of shared resources.

__F__   3. A cost pool is a grouping of individual costs the total of which is allocated using several allocation bases.

__T__   4. An overriding concern in forming a cost pool is to ensure that the costs in the pool are homogeneous or similar.

__F__   5. Service departments provide both direct manufacturing activity and indirect support.

__T__   6. It is generally a good idea to allocate budgeted rather than actual service department costs.

__F__   7. Cost allocation is not required in a responsibility accounting system.

__T__   8. Most accountants believe that managers should be held responsible only for cost they can control.

__T__   9. Various allocation bases may be equally justifiable but may result in substantially different allocations.

__F__   10. Assigning overhead to products using a small number of overhead cost pools has the benefit of being simple and avoiding distortion of product cost.

__F__   11. A major benefit of using ABC costing systems is that ABC is less likely than traditional costing systems to overcost complex, low-volume products and undercost simple, high-volume products.

__F__   12. ABM and ABC have the same primary goals.

Chapter 5 – Key Terms Matching

Match the terms found in Chapter 5 with the following definitions:

a. ability to bear costs approach to allocation
b. activity-based management
c. cost allocation
d. cost driver
e. cost objective
f. cost pool

g. direct method of allocation
h. equity approach to allocation
i. lump-sum allocation
j. relative benefits approach to allocation
k. responsibility accounting system
l. unitized fixed costs

_K_ 1. A system of accounting that traces revenues and costs to organizational units and individuals with related responsibility for generating revenue and controlling costs.

_D_ 2. A measure of the activity, related to a cost pool, that is used to allocate cost.

_G_ 3. A method of allocating service department costs to production departments which does not allow for allocation of costs among service departments.

_A_ 4. The notion in cost allocation that the allocation base should result in more costs being allocated to products, services, or departments that are more profitable.

_C_ 5. The process of assigning indirect costs.

_I_ 6. Allocations of fixed costs in which predetermined amounts are allocated regardless of changes in the level of activity.

_L_ 7. Fixed costs stated on a per unit basis.

_B_ 8. A management approach that involves analyzing and costing activities with the goal of improving efficiency and effectiveness.

_E_ 9. The object of cost allocation.

_h_ 10. An attempt to allocate costs in a way that is fair to interested parties.

_J_ 11. The notion in cost allocation that the allocation base should result in more costs being allocated to the cost objectives that benefit most from incurring the cost.

_F_ 12. A grouping of overhead costs based on the major activity that created them.

Chapter 5 – Multiple Choice

1. Which of the following is not a reason why firms allocate costs?
    a. To calculate the full cost of products for GAAP reporting
    b. To punish managers for using resources inefficiently
    c. To provide information for decision making
    d. All of the above are reasons why firms allocate costs

2. Cost-plus contracts:
    a. often include not only manufacturing costs but also a share of general and administrative costs.
    b. require a substantial amount of cost allocation to assign indirect manufacturing and indirect general and administrative cost to the contract work.
    c. both a and b.
    d. neither a nor b.

3. The overriding concern in forming a cost pool is to ensure that:
    a. only production department costs are allocated.
    b. only service department costs are allocated.
    c. the costs in the pool are homogeneous.
    d. the number of cost pools is small.

4. Which of the following is not an approach to cost allocation?
    a. Contribution margin
    b. Ability to bear costs
    c. Relative benefits
    d. Cause-and-effect relationship

5. In a furniture manufacturing firm, which of the following would not be considered a production department?
    a. Assembly
    b. Personnel
    c. Packaging
    d. All of the above would be considered to be production departments.

6. The three steps in the cost allocation process are:
    a. form cost pools, select an allocation base, identify cost objectives
    b. identify cost objectives, select and allocation base, form cost pools
    c. select an allocation base, form cost pools, identify cost objectives
    d. identify cost objectives, form cost pools, select an allocation base

7. Allocation of fixed cost sometimes make the fixed cost appear to be variable. Which of the following allocation methods remedies this problem?
    a. Lump-sum allocations of fixed costs
    b. Long-run allocations of fixed costs
    c. Changes in activity allocation of fixed costs
    d. None of the above

8.   Harper Manufacturing Company has two production departments, Assembly and Packaging, and two service departments, maintenance and personnel. Maintenance costs for the period total $20,000 while personnel costs total $9,000. All service department costs are allocated based on number of employees. Assembly has 1,000 employees, Packaging has 1,500 employees, maintenance has 100 employees, and personnel has 80 employees. The amount of personnel costs allocated to Assembly using the direct method will be:
   a. $3,600.
   b. $3,358.
   c. $3,462.
   d. $9,000.

9.   Which of the following is a problem brought about when allocating costs?
   a.   Allocations of costs that are not controllable
   b.   Use of only volume-related allocation bases
   c.   Both a and b
   d.   None of the above are problems

10.   Which of the following is not a benefit of ABC?
   a.   ABC is less likely than traditional costing systems to undercost complex, low-volume products
   b.   ABC is less likely than traditional costing systems to overcost simple, high-volume products.
   c.   ABC may lead to improvements in cost control.
   d.   ABC is less expensive than traditional costing systems.

11.   A primary goal of AMB is:
   a.   ABM focuses on activities with the goal of measuring the costs of products and services produced by them.
   b.   ABM focuses on activities with the goal of managing the activities themselves.
   c.   both a and b are primary goals of AMB.
   d.   neither a nor b are primary goals of ABM.

12.   A problem with the relative benefits approach to allocating costs is:
   a.   fixed costs being allocated to departments that do not use the allocated resource.
   b.   fixed costs being allocated to departments that did not exist when the resource was acquired.
   c.   fixed costs being allocated to departments that are most profitable.
   d.   both a and b.

Exercise 5 – 1   The following data relates to the three retail departments of Upper Echelon Department Store – Clothing, Housewares, and Fine Jewelry.

	Clothing	Housewares	Fine Jewelry
Square footage occupied	12,000	9,000	3,000
Dollar volume of sales	$1,000,000	$800,000	$2,200,000

The janitorial department for the Upper Echelon has budgeted annual costs of $400,000 based on the expected operating level for the coming year. Upper Echelon is considering two allocation bases for assignment of cost to departments – square footage occupied and dollar volume of sales.

1.   Allocate the expense of the janitorial department to the three retail departments using square feet of space occupied as an allocation base.

$$AR = \frac{400,000}{24,000} = 16.67$$

Clothing – 12,000 × 16.67 = $200,000.00

Housewares – 9,000 × 16.67 = $150,000.00

Fine Jewelry – 3,000 × 16.67 = $50,010.00

2.   Allocate the expense of the janitorial department to the three retail departments using dollar volume of sales as an allocation base.

$$AR = \frac{400,000}{4,000,000.00} = 0.10$$

Clothing – 100,000

Housewares – 80,000

Fine Jewelry – 220,000

3.   The president of Upper Echelon has asked managers of the three retail departments to meet and decide which allocation base to use. Assuming you are the manager of the Fine Jewelry Department, which allocation base would you find preferable and why? Would your answer be different if you were manager of Housewares? Why?

I would use the square footage method.

Housewares would prefer sales

Fine Jewelry would prefer the square footage method

Exercise 5 – 2 The Merry Heart Drug Company, manufacturer of a number of pharmaceutical products, has two production departments: Prescription Drugs and Over the Counter Drugs. In addition, Merry Heart has two service departments – Human Resources and Janitorial. Based on the expected operating level for the coming year, Human Resources has budgeted cost of $420,000 and Janitorial has budgeted costs of $600,000. Cost accumulated in Human Resources is allocated based on the number of employees, while cost accumulated in Janitorial is allocated based on the square feet of space occupied. The following data relate to Merry Heart's production departments.

	Number of Employees	Square Feet Occupied
Prescription Drugs	800	95,000
Over the Counter Drugs	1,200	205,000

Allocate the service department cost to the production departments using the direct method.

	Prescription Department	Over The Counter Department
Human Resources	168,000	252,000
Janitorial	190,000	410,000
	358,000	662,000

BUDGETED COSTS

H/R => $420,000/year   Based on # Employees

Janitorial => $600,000/year   Based on square feet of space occupied

Exercise 5 – 3 McMeekan Memorial Hospital has three divisions – General Hospital, Oncology, and Laboratory. In addition, McMeekan has three service departments – Janitorial Services, Food Services, and Administrative Services. The three service departments have the following budgeted costs and allocation bases:

			OH RATE
Janitorial Services	$ 800,000	Square feet occupied	4.0
Food Services	2,560,000	Meals served	2.56
Administrative Services	4,892,000	Number of patients	8.153

Using the following data, allocate the service department costs to General Hospital, Oncology, and Laboratory using the direct method.

	Square Feet Occupied	Meals Served	Number of Patients
General Hospital	150,000	440,000	240,000
Oncology	20,000	30,000	30,000
Laboratory	30,000	530,000	330,000

	General Hospital	Oncology	Laboratory
Janitorial Services	600,000	80,000	120,000
Food ~~Oncology~~			
ADM. SVCS ~~Laboratory~~			
Total			

Problem 5 – 4   Although he is quite happy in University City, Porter Roberts returns to his home town once a month to visit with his family. While in Home City, Porter arranges to have dinner with three of his closest friends from high school, Allison Westland, Forrest Kaiser, and Elizabeth Push. Suffering from wanderlust, Porter always puts the bill on his American Express card so that he can accumulate frequent flier points. The four friends then split the bill equally. Porter has begun to grow uncomfortable with this arrangement because one of the friends tends to eat and drink more than others in the group. The bill for the most recent dinner reflects the following costs per diner.

Friend	Entrée	Dessert	Beverages	Total	Diff
Westland	$24	$ 7	$29	$60	21.50
Kaiser	15	6	18	39	0.50
Push	21	8	0	29	-9.50
Roberts	16	6	4	26	-12.50
			57	154	

1.   What is the average cost of the meal?

$38.5

2.   Since the bill was split equally, did some of the friends pay too much while others did not pay enough?   Which friends paid too much and which friends paid too little and by how much?

3.   Why is this problem in this chapter?

Problem 5 – 5   Mr. Regork owns a large grocery store in a metropolitan area. For twenty years, the accountant has applied overhead to the various departments – produce, meat, dairy, canned goods, bakery, and floral – based on the basis of employee hours worked. Mr. Regork's son who is an accounting student at a local university has suggested his father should consider activity based costing (ABC). In an attempt to implement ABC Mr. Regork and his son have identified the following activities. They needs your help in determining a cost driver for each of the activities.

	Cost Pool	**Cost Driver**
a.	Placing orders	# OF ORDERS
b.	Checking out customers	# OF CUSTOMERS
c.	Bagging groceries	# of customers / # per sales
d.	Delivering groceries	# of orders
e.	Stocking shelves	Hours wanted stocking
f.	Janitorial and Maintenance	Square feet occupied
g.	Training employees	# OF EMPLOYEES
h.	Administrative	Dollar volume of sales
i.	Advertising and Marketing	# OF AD campaigns
j.	Accounting and Legal Services	Dollar volume of sales

Solutions – Chapter 5 – True/False

1. F From a decision-making standpoint, the allocated cost should measure the opportunity cost of using a company resource.
2. T
3. F A cost pool is a grouping of individual costs whose total is allocated using one allocation base.
4. T
5. F Production departments engage in direct manufacturing activities; service departments provide indirect support.
6. T
7. F Cost allocation is required because one organizational unit is often responsible for the costs incurred by another organizational unit.
8. T
9. T
10. F Assigning overhead to products using a small number of overhead cost pools has the benefit of being simple, however, product cost may be seriously distorted.
11. F A major benefit of using ABC costing systems is that ABC is less likely than traditional costing systems to undercost complex, low-volume products and overcost simple, high volume products.
12. F While ABC focuses on activities with the goal of measuring the costs of products and services produced by them, ABM focuses on activities with the goal of managing the activities themselves.

Solutions – Key Terms Matching

1. k. relative benefits approach
2. d. cost driver
3. g. direct method
4. a. ability to bear costs
5. c. cost allocation
6. i. lump-sum allocation
7. l. unitized fixed costs
8. b. activity-based management
9. e. cost objective
10. h. equity approach
11. j. relative benefits approach
12. f. cost pool

Solutions – Multiple Choice

1. b
2. c
3. c
4. a
5. b
6. d
7. a
8. a
9. c
10. d
11. b
12. b

Solution – Exercise 5-1 The following data relates to the three retail departments of Upper Echelon Department Store – Clothing, Housewares, and Fine Jewelry.

	Clothing	Housewares	Fine Jewelry
Square footage occupied	12,000	9,000	3,000
Dollar volume of sales	$1,000,000	$800,000	$2,200,000

The janitorial department for the Upper Echelon has budgeted annual costs of $400,000 based on the expected operating level for the coming year. Upper Echelon is considering two allocation bases for assignment of cost to departments – square footage occupied and dollar volume of sales.

1. Allocate the expense of the janitorial department to the three retail departments using square feet of space occupied as an allocation base.

$$12,000 \div 24,000 = 50\% \quad \times \$400,000 = \$200,000 \text{ to Clothing}$$
$$9,000 \div 24,000 = 37.5\% \quad \times \$400,000 = \$150,000 \text{ to Housewares}$$
$$\underline{3,000} \div 24,000 = 12.5\% \quad \times \$400,000 = \underline{\$\ 50,000} \text{ to Fine Jewelry}$$
$$\underline{24,000} \qquad\qquad \underline{100\%} \qquad\qquad \underline{\$400,000}$$

2. Allocate the expense of the janitorial department to the three retail departments using dollar volume of sales as an allocation base.

$$\$1,000,000 \div 4,000,000 = 25\% \times \$400,000 = \$100,000$$
$$800,000 \div 4,000,000 = 20\% \times \ \ 400,000 = \ \ 80,000$$
$$\underline{2,200,000} \div 4,000,000 = \underline{55\%} \times \ \ 400,000 = \underline{220,000}$$
$$\underline{\$4,000,000} \qquad\qquad \underline{100\%} \qquad\qquad \underline{\$400,000}$$

3. The president of Upper Echelon has asked managers of the three retail departments to meet and decide which allocation base to use. Assuming you are the manager of the Fine Jewelry Department, which allocation base would you find preferable and why? Would your answer be different if you were manager of Housewares? Why?

The manager of Fine Jewelry would want to use square footage occupied as the allocation base. The square footage occupied by Fine Jewelry is relatively small compared to the other departments, whereas the dollar volume of sales is large relative to the other departments. Therefore, the amount of janitorial cost assigned to Fine Jewelry would be less using square footage occupied.

Yes, the manager of Housewares would want to use dollar volume of sales. The dollar volume of sales for Housewares is small relative to the other departments. Therefore Housewares would have less janitorial cost assigned using dollar volume of sales.

Solution – Exercise 5 – 2

The Merry Heart Drug Company, manufacturer of a number of pharmaceutical products, has two production departments: Prescription Drugs and Over the Counter Drugs. In addition, Merry Heart has two service departments – Human Resources and Janitorial. Based on the expected operating level for the coming year, Human Resources has budgeted cost of $420,000 and Janitorial has budgeted costs of $600,000. Cost accumulated in Human Resources is allocated based on the number of employees, while cost accumulated in Janitorial is allocated based on the square feet of space occupied. The following data relate to Merry Heart's production departments.

	Number of Employees	Square Feet Occupied
Prescription Drugs	800	95,000
Over the Counter Drugs	1,200	205,000

Allocate the service department cost to the production departments using the direct method.

	Prescription Department	Over The Counter Department
Human Resources	$168,000	$252,000
Janitorial	270,000	330,000
Total	$438,000	$285,000

$$800 \div 2,000 = 40\% \times \$420,000 = \$168,000$$
$$1,200 \div 2,000 = 60\% \times 420,000 = 252,000$$
$$2,000 \qquad 100\% \qquad\qquad \$420,000$$

$$135,000 \div 300,000 = 45\% \times \$600,000 = \$270,000$$
$$165,000 \div 300,000 = 55\% \times \$600,000 = 330,000$$
$$300,000 \qquad\qquad 100\% \qquad\qquad \$600,000$$

Solution – Exercise 5 – 3

McMeekan Memorial Hospital has three divisions – General Hospital, Oncology, and Laboratory. In addition, McMeekan has three service departments – Janitorial Services, Food Services, and Administrative Services. The three service departments have the following budgeted costs and allocation bases:

Janitorial Services	$ 80,000	Square feet occupied
Food Services	256,000	Meals served
Administrative Services	489,200	Number of patients

Using the following data, allocate the service department costs to General Hospital, Oncology, and Laboratory using the direct method.

	Square Feet Occupied	Meals Served	Number of Patients
General Hospital	150,000	440,000	240,000
Oncology	20,000	30,000	30,000
Laboratory	30,000	530,000	330,000

	General Hospital	Oncology	Laboratory
Janitorial Services	$ 60,000	$ 8,000	$ 12,000
Food Services	112,640	7,680	135,680
Administrative Services	195,680	24,460	269,060
Total	$368,320	$40,140	$416,740

Janitorial Services

150,000 ÷ 200,000 = 75% × $80,000 = 60,000
20,000 ÷ 200,000 = 10% × 80,000 = 8,000
30,000 ÷ 200,000 = 15% × 80,000 = 12,000
200,000   100% $80,000

Food Services

440,000 ÷ 1,000,000 = 44% × $256,000 =$112,640
30,000 ÷ 1,000,000 = 3% × 256,000 =   7,680
530,000 ÷ 1,000,000 = 53% × 256,000 = 135,680
1,000,000   100% $256.000

Administrative Services

240,000 ÷ 600,000 = 40% × $489,200 = $195,680
30,000 ÷ 600,000 = 5% × 489,200 =   24,460
330,000 ÷ 600,000 = 55% × 489,200 = 269,060
600,000   100% $489,200

Solution – Problem 5 – 4

Although he is quite happy in University City, Porter Roberts returns to his home town once a month to visit with his family. While in Home City, Porter arranges to have dinner with three of his closest friends from high school, Allison Westland, Forrest Kaiser, and Elizabeth Push. Suffering from wanderlust, Porter always puts the bill on his American Express card so that he can accumulate frequent flier points. The four friends then split the bill equally. Porter has begun to grow uncomfortable with this arrangement because one of the friends tends to eat and drink more than others in the group. The bill for the most recent dinner reflects the following costs per diner.

Friend	Entrée	Dessert	Beverages	Total
Westland	$24	$ 7	$29	$60
Kaiser	15	6	18	39
Push	21	8	0	29
Roberts	16	6	4	26
	$76	$27	$51	$154

1.   What is the average cost of the meal? $154 ÷ 4 = $38.50

2.   Since the bill was split equally, did some of the friends pay too much while others did not pay enough?   Which friends paid too much and which friends paid too little and by how much?

Westland's share $60.00 paid $38.50 – underpaid $21.50

Kaiser's share $39.00 paid $38.50 – underpaid $ .50

Push's share $29.00 paid $38.50 – overpaid $9.50

Roberts' share $26.00 paid $38.50 – overpaid $12.50

3.   Why is this problem in this chapter?

To illustrate the point that arbitrary allocations or assignment of cost can be very unfair.

Solution – Problem 5 – 5 Mr. Regork owns a large grocery store in a metropolitan area. For twenty years, the accountant has applied overhead to the various departments – produce, meat, dairy, canned goods, bakery, and floral – based on the basis of employee hours worked. Mr. Regork's son who is an accounting student at a local university has suggested his father should consider activity based costing (ABC). In an attempt to implement ABC Mr. Regork and his son have identified the following activities. They need your help in determining a cost driver for each of the activities.

	Cost Pool	Cost Driver(s)
a.	Placing orders	number or orders
b.	Checking out customers	number of customers dollar volume of sales
c.	Bagging groceries	number of customers dollar volume of sales
d.	Delivering groceries	number of delivery orders
e.	Stocking shelves	hours worked stocking
f.	Janitorial and Maintenance	square feet occupied
g.	Training employees	total number of employees number of new employees
h.	Administrative	dollar volume of sales
i.	Advertising and Marketing	number of ad campaigns
j.	Accounting Services	dollar volume of sales

CHAPTER **6**

The Use of Cost Information in Management Decision Making

CHAPTER INTRODUCTION

Before making decisions, managers must gain a thorough understanding of the cost information that is relevant. Previous chapters have examined various issues involving costs. This chapter discusses the topic of how cost information is used by managers in decision making.

Objectives, Terms, and Discussions

LO1   *Explain the role of incremental analysis (analysis of incremental costs and revenues) in management decisions.*

All decisions involve a choice among alternative courses of action. The solution to all business problem involves incremental analysis—the analysis of the incremental revenue generated and the incremental costs incurred when one decision alternative is chosen over another. **Incremental revenue** is the additional revenue received as a result of selecting one decision alternative over another. **Incremental cost** (also referred to as relevant cost or differential cost) is the additional cost incurred as a result of selecting one decision alternative over another. Incremental costs are also referred to as **relevant costs** because they are the only costs that are relevant to consider when analyzing decision alternatives or **differential costs** because they are the costs that differ between decision alternatives. If an alternative generates an incremental profit (incremental revenue less incremental costs) then it should be selected. This chapter discusses the use of incremental analysis for several decision settings:

- The decision to make or buy a product
- The decision to drop a product line
- The decision to engage in additional processing of a product

In some cases, a company may purchase one or more of the components of manufactured goods from another company. This may lead to considerable savings if the outside supplier can offer the component at a reasonable price. Two decision alternatives arise in this situation: make or buy the component. No incremental revenues are involved. The analysis of this decision concentrates solely on incremental costs. An **opportunity cost**—the value of benefits foregone by selecting one decision alternative over another—must be considered in decision making.

Dropping a product line is a very significant decision and one that receives a great deal of attention. The proper approach to analyzing this problem is to calculate the change in income that will result from dropping the product line. If income will increase without the product, the product line should be dropped. If income will decrease if the product is eliminated, the product line should be kept. Comparison of incremental revenues and costs that result from dropping the product line should be made. Fixed costs are not always irrelevant costs. Some fixed costs are **avoidable costs**—cost that can be avoided if a particular action is undertaken. Allocated fixed cost, also referred to as **common costs**, are generally not avoidable. Thus, no cost savings will be achieved with respect to common costs. When analyzing a decision involving dropping a product or service, remember that common fixed costs are not incremental. This will allow you to avoid what is sometimes referred to as the **cost allocation death spiral**. Products or services may not appear to be profitable because they receive allocations of common fixed costs. If the product or service is dropped, those common fixed costs will not be reduced or eliminated, but will be allocated to the remaining products and services. The additional allocation of fixed costs may result in the remaining products appearing to be unprofitable.

Sometimes, incremental analysis is used when manufacturers must decide whether to sell a product in a partially completed stage or incur the additional processing costs required to complete the product. Should the manufacturer sell the products in their current partial state of completion for a lesser price, or should the additional processing cost be incurred? First, incremental revenue should be examined. Incremental revenue is simply the difference in revenue between the two alternatives. Next incremental costs should be examined. Recall that sunk costs (costs incurred in the past) are not incremental costs since they will not increase or decrease with the choice of one alternative over another. Incremental cost is the difference in costs between the two alternatives.

LO2   *Define sunk cost, avoidable cost, and opportunity cost and understand how to use these concepts in analyzing decisions.*

The basic approach to decision making is to compare decisions in terms of costs and revenues that are incremental. Costs that can be *avoided* by taking a particular course of action are always incremental costs and are relevant to the analysis of a decision. Costs that are sunk—costs that are already incurred and not reversible—are never incremental costs and are not relevant to the analysis of a decision. Fixed costs may be sunk and irrelevant (not incremental costs); they may not be sunk but still be irrelevant; or they may not be sunk and may be relevant. Finally, opportunity costs represent the benefit foregone by selecting a particular decision alternative over another. They are always incremental costs, and must be considered when making a decision.

LO3   *Analyze decisions involving joint costs.*

When two or more products result from common inputs, they are known as **joint products**. The costs of common inputs are referred to as **joint costs**. The stage of production at which individual products are identified is referred to as the **split-off point**. Beyond this point each product may undergo further separate processing and may incur additional costs.

For financial reporting purposes, the cost of the common inputs must be allocated to the joint products. The total joint cost will be incurred no matter what the company does with the joint products beyond the split-off point. Joint costs are not incremental to production of an individual joint product beyond the split-off point. Thus, they are irrelevant to any decision regarding an individual joint product. The joint cost is relevant to decisions involving the joint products as a group.

Joint cost may be allocated using the **relative sales value method**. With this method, the amount of joint cost allocated to products depends on the relative sales value of the products at the split-off point.

$$\text{Joint cost allocated to Product A} = \frac{\text{Sales value of A}}{\text{Sales value of A} + \text{Sales value of B}} \times \text{Joint Cost}$$

$$\text{Joint cost allocated to Product B} = \frac{\text{Sales value of B}}{\text{Sales value of A} + \text{Sales value of B}} \times \text{Joint Cost}$$

LO4   *Discuss the importance of qualitative considerations in management decisions.*

Qualitative aspects of decision situations must receive the same careful attention as the quantitative components. For instance, in a make or buy decision, some qualitative considerations would be loss of control if items are purchased, reduced morale if jobs are lost, and possible future downturns in demand.

LOA1   *Calculate a price based on marking up costs.*

Many companies use cost-plus pricing. With a cost-plus approach, the company starts with an estimate of the cost and adds a markup to arrive at a price that allows for a reasonable level of profit. An advantage of a cost-plus approach is that it is simple to apply. Another advantage is that the company will earn a reasonable profit if a sufficient quantity of the product can be sold at the specified selling price. A limitation of this approach is the difficulty in determining an appropriate markup percentage. Another problem is that cost-plus pricing is inherently circular. Demand must be estimated to determine fixed cost per unit. However price (which includes fixed costs) affects demand.

LOA2   *Perform incremental analysis for a special order.*

Generally, products are not sold for a price less than their full cost. However, it may be beneficial to charge a lower price when companies are faced with special orders from customers. If accepting the order will not affect demand for its other products, a company may choose to accept the offer. The special order decision presents two alternatives: accept or reject the special order. The most obvious incremental item is the revenue associated with the special order. In addition, direct material, direct labor, and variable overhead are incremental costs since they will not be incurred if the order is rejected. Generally, fixed cost will not change and are, therefore, irrelevant.

LOA3   *Explain how to consider demand in setting prices.*

Cost is half of the product pricing equation. Demand is the other half. Prices should not be set based only on a consideration of cost. Managers also need to consider the quantities that will be demanded at various prices. If managers can estimate customer demand at various prices, determining the optimal prices is relatively straightforward. Subtract variable costs from price to obtain the contribution margin, multiply the contribution margin by demand, subtract fixed costs, and estimate profit. The price with the highest profit should be selected.

Review of Key Terms

Avoidable cost: Costs that can be avoided if a company takes a particular action.

Common cost: Cost incurred for the benefit of multiple departments or products.

Differential cost: Costs that differ between decision alternatives.

Incremental cost: Costs that increase or decrease if a decision alternative is selected.

Incremental revenue: Revenue that increases or decreases if a decision alternative is selected.

Joint cost: The costs of the common inputs that result in two or more products.

Joint products: Two or more products that arise from common inputs.

Opportunity cost: The values of benefits foregone by selecting one decision alternative over another.

Relative sales value method: A method of allocating joint costs in which the allocation is based on the relative sales value of the products at the split-off point.

Relevant cost: The only cost items managers need to consider when analyzing decision alternatives because they differ among decision alternatives.

Split-off point: Stage of production where joint products are individually identifiable.

Chapter 6 – True/False

_T_ 1. The solution to all business problems involves incremental analysis.

_F_ 2. Incremental costs are also referred to as sunk costs.

_T_ 3. In a make or buy decision, incremental revenue is not involved in the decision.

_F_ 4. Opportunity costs are not relevant and are not considered in decision making.

_F_ 5. Fixed costs are never relevant and are not considered in decision making.

_F_ 6. Sunk costs are never relevant and are not considered in decision making.

_T_ 7. For financial reporting purposes, the cost of the common inputs must be allocated to the joint products.

_F_ 8. Joint costs are incremental to production of an individual joint product.

_F_ 9. Using the relative sales value method, the amount of joint cost allocated to products depends on the relative sales value of the products at the final stage of production

_F_ 10. Qualitative aspects of decision situations need not be considered in decision making.

_T_ 11. A limitation of using cost-plus pricing is that it is inherently circular.

_T_ 12. Cost is half of the product pricing equation. Profit is the other half.

Chapter 6 – Key Terms Matching

Match the terms, found in Chapter 6, with the following definitions:

a. avoidable cost
b. common cost
c. differential cost
d. incremental cost
e. incremental revenue
f. joint cost

g. joint products
h. opportunity cost
i. relative sales value method
j. relevant cost
k. split-off point

_____ D _____ 1. Costs that increase or decrease if a decision alternative is selected.

_____ A _____ 2. Costs that can be avoided if a company takes a particular action.

_____ k _____ 3. Stage of production where joint product are individually identifiable.

_____ I _____ 4. A method of allocating joint costs in which the allocation is based on the relative sales value of the products at the split-off point.

_____ E _____ 5. Revenue that increases or decreases if a decision alternative is selected.

_____ G _____ 6. Two or more products that arise from common inputs.

_____ B _____ 7. Cost incurred for the benefit of multiple departments or products.

_____ F _____ 8. The costs of the common inputs that result in two or more products.

_____ h _____ 9. The values of benefits foregone by selecting one decision alternative over another.

_____ J _____ 10. The only cost items managers need to consider when analyzing decision alternatives because they differ among decision alternatives.

_____ C _____ 11. Costs that differ between decision alternatives.

Chapter 6 – Multiple Choice

1.   Which of the following would not be classified as an incremental cost in a make or buy decision?
    a.   Avoidable cost
    b.   Opportunity cost
    c.   Sunk cost
    d.   Both b and c

2.   Rose Company produces 1,000 units each year that are used as a component in one of its products. The unit cost is made up of variable manufacturing costs of $3.75 and fixed manufacturing costs of $3. The unit can be purchased from an outside source for $5. If the part is purchased, $2 of the fixed costs will be eliminated. What is the effect on net operating income from purchasing the part from an outside source?
    a. $1,750 decrease
    b. $2,000 increase
    c. $750 increase
    d.   None of the above

3.   Which of the following would not be an example of a common cost?
    a.   The salary of an assembly-line worker paid by the hour
    b.   Rent on factory building
    c.   The salary of the owner/manager of a manufacturing firm
    d.   Both a and c

4.   Which of the following businesses would have joint costs?
    a.   Dairy processing businesses
    b.   Lumber companies
    c.   Fuel companies
    d.   A, b, and c would have joint costs

5.   Depreciation on equipment already purchased is:
    a.   not sunk and irrelevant.
    b.   sunk and irrelevant.
    c.   not sunk and relevant.
    d.   sunk and relevant.

Products Widget and Wadnet are joint products. The joint production cost of the products is $1,500. Widget has a market value of $700 at the split-off point. If Widget is further processed at an additional cost of $300, its market value is $1,200. Product Wadnet has a market value of $1,400 at the split-off point. If Product Wadnet is further processed at an additional cost of $300, its market value is $1,500. Use the information to answer questions 6 and 7.

6.   Using the relative sales value method, calculate the joint production cost that will be allocated to Widget and Wadnet.
    a. $500 to Widget; $1,000 to Wadnet
    b. $666 to Widget; $834 to Wadnet
    c. $750 to Widget; $750 to Wadnet
    d.   None of the above

7.   Should Product Widget and Wadnet be further processed?
     a.   Widget, no; Wadnet, yes
     b.   Widget, yes, Wadnet, yes
     c.   Widget, yes, Wadnet, no
     d.   Widget, no, Wadnet, no

8.   Which of the following is not a qualitative consideration in the context of a make or buy decision?
     a.   The adverse effect of a downturn in business is less severe when using an outside supplier.
     b.   The adverse effect on employee moral if jobs are lost due to using an outside supplier.
     c.   The loss of control over the production process due to using an outside supplier.
     d.   The avoidance of a major payroll cost due to using an outside supplier.

9.   Sweet Emily's Candy Shop has received a special order for 1,200 brownies. The customer has offered a price of $6 per dozen. The unit cost of a brownie, at its normal sales level of 20,000 per year is variable production cost of $.33, fixed production costs of $.25, variable selling costs $.10, and fixed selling and administrative costs $.15. There is ample idle capacity to produce the special order without any change in unit costs except that variable selling costs would be $.05. How would accepting the special order affect Sweet Emily's net operating income?
     a. $336 decrease
     b. $144 increase
     c. $24 increase
     d.   None of the above

10. One of Noah Company's products has a total contribution margin of $5,000 and total fixed costs of $6,000. If the product is dropped, $2,000 of the fixed costs will be eliminated. If the product is dropped, what will be the effect on Noah's net income?
     a.   Increase by $2,000
     b.   Decrease by $2,000
     c.   Increase by $3,000
     d.   Decrease by $3,000

11. The cost allocation death spiral is created when:
     a.   products are not allocated any fixed costs.
     b.   when fixed costs are considered to be sunk costs.
     c.   products receive allocations of common fixed costs
     d.   when products are not allocated any variable costs.

12. An example of a fixed cost that is incremental is:
     a.   salary of a supervisor who will be retained if decision alternative A is made and fired if decision alternative B is made.
     b.   salary of a supervisor who will be retained if regardless of the decision alternative chosen.
     c.   rent on factory warehouse space already in use.
     d.   direct material.

Exercise 6 – 1 Will Wash, Manager of the Laundry Department at the Hooty Snooty Hotel is considering the purchase of a dryer which turns off automatically when laundry is dry. The new dryer will replace a dryer currently being used, which must be monitored to determine when laundry is dry. Selected information on the two machines is given below:

	Standard Dryer	Automatic Turn-off Dryer
Original cost new	$6,000	$8,000
Accumulated depreciation to date	2,400	- 0 -
Current salvage value	2,000	- 0 -
Estimated cost per year to operate	4,500	2,500
Remaining years of useful life	5 years	5 years

Required:

Prepare a computation covering the five-year period that will show the net advantage or disadvantage of purchasing the automatic dryer. Ignore income taxes, and use only relevant costs in your analysis.

Exercise 6 – 2 Golden Years Inc. operates three retirement facilities and expects the following results for the coming year.

	The Oaks	The Pines	The Elms	Total
Revenue	$100,000	$150,000	$180,000	$430,000
Variable costs	45,000	60,000	60,000	165,000
Contribution margin	55,000	90,000	120,000	265,000
Fixed costs	80,000	50,000	60,000	190,000
Net income (loss)	($ 25,000)	$ 40,000	$ 60,000	$ 75,000

Answer each of the following questions independently.

1.   Fixed costs are all allocated and unavoidable. What will happen to profit if Golden Years discontinues operations at The Oaks?

2.   Suppose now that $25,000 of the fixed costs shown for the Oaks are avoidable. What will happen to total profits if Golden Years discontinues operations at The Oaks?

Exercise 6 – 3 Joe College graduated from a university that is located three hours from the city in which he now works. A loyal alumnus and an avid football fan, Joe always buys season tickets to the football games although his Alma Mater has posted loosing records in each of the last three years. Joe sends a check for $218 to the University by July 1 of every year to cover the cost of two tickets for each of the 7 home games plus $50 for a parking permit. Joe has difficulty finding friends to accompany him to the games. However, he is adamant that he must go to the games because he has paid for the tickets. Friends insist that the cost of the tickets is a sunk cost and that the decision should be based on future costs that would be different between alternatives – going to the game and not going to the game. Friends have calculated the fuel for the 6-hour round trip costs $15.00 and two means while away from home for the game can easily cost $30 or more. Write a memo to Joe outlining the relevant costs associated with a trip to the game.

Problem 6 – 4 Chip Drayer has just inherited a peanut farm from his father. Chip estimates that he can produce 10,000 pounds of peanuts for approximately $12,500 per pound. Chip can sell the peanuts as they come from the field for $2.00 per pound. Alternatively, Chip can have the peanuts processed further at a cost of $0.15 per pound and sell them as roasted peanuts for $2.50.

1.   Define joint cost.

2.   What is the joint cost associated with producing the peanuts?

3.   Define split-off point.

4.   Should Chip sell the peanuts for $2.00 as they come from the field or process the peanuts further and sell them at$2.50 as roasted peanuts? Provide figures to support your conclusion.

Problem 6 – 5 The Paz Company makes an electric skateboard-like scooter that is small enough to fit into a school locker. Production for the year 2004 is budgeted at 20,000 scooters. Currently, Paz makes all of the parts for manufacturing the scooter. However, an outside source has offered to make and sell Paz 20,000 steering columns for $90 each. The controller of Paz has researched the cost to produce the steering column in house and has found the following cost structure:

Variable costs	
Direct materials	$48
Direct labor	23
Overhead	16
Total variable cost per unit	87

Fixed costs of $40,000 represents depreciation on a special equipment designed to make the steering columns. This equipment cannot be used for any other purpose. The supervisory salary of $50,000 is for the supervisor of the assembly line where the steering columns are made. The supervisor is not involved with the manufacture of any other parts. Therefore, his salary can be eliminated if the steering columns are purchased. The other fixed costs are allocated costs and cannot be eliminated. Help the controller evaluate the offer to purchase by completing the schedules below.

Incremental Cost Analysis
Paz Company
Make or Buy Decision

	Cost of Making Units	Cost of Buying Units	Incremental Cost (Savings)
Variable costs			
Direct material	960,000		
Direct labor	460,000		
Variable overhead	320,000		
Total variable costs	1,740,000		
Fixed Costs			
Depreciation	40,000	40,000	
Supervisory salary	50,000		
Other	2,000	2,000	
Total fixed costs	92,000	42,000	
Cost of buying units		1,800,000	
Total	$ 1,832,000	1,842,000	

Incremental Cost Analysis
Paz Company

Cost of buying (20,000 units @ $ 90)		1,800,000
Cost savings (avoidable if purchase units outside):		
Variable costs	1,740,000	
Other		
Excess cost of buying units from an outside vender		

Solutions – Chapter 6 – True/False

1. T
2. F   Incremental costs are also referred to as relevant costs or differential costs.
3. T
4. F   Opportunity costs are relevant and must be considered in decision making.
5. F   Fixed costs can be sunk and irrelevant, not sunk and irrelevant, or not sunk and relevant.
6. T
7. T
8. F   Joint costs are not incremental to production of an individual joint product.
9. F   Using the relative sales value method, the amount of joint cost allocated to products depends on the relative sales value of the products at the split-off point.
10. F   Qualitative aspects of decision situations must receive the same attention as quantitative components.
11. T
12. F   Cost is half of the product equation. Demand is the other half.

Solutions – Chapter 6 – Key Terms Matching

1.	d. incremental cost		7.	b. common cost
2.	a. avoidable cost		8.	f. joint cost
3.	k. split-off point		9.	h. opportunity cost
4.	i. relative sales value method		10.	j. relevant cost
5.	e. incremental revenue		11.	c. differential cost
6.	g. joint products			

Solutions – Chapter 6 – Multiple Choice

1.	c		7.	c
2.	c		8.	d
3.	a		9.	b
4.	d		10.	d
5.	b		11.	c
6.	a		12.	a

Solution – Exercise 6 – 1 Will Wash, Manager of the Laundry Department at the Hooty Snooty Hotel is considering the purchase of a dryer which turns off automatically when laundry is dry. The new dryer will replace a dryer currently being used, which must be monitored to determine when laundry is dry. Selected information on the two machines is given below:

	Standard Dryer	Automatic Turn-off Dryer
Original cost new	$6,000	$8,000
Accumulated depreciation to date	2,400	- 0 -
Current salvage value	2,000	- 0 -
Estimated cost per year to operate	4,500	2,500
Remaining years of useful life	5 years	5 years

Required:

Prepare a computation covering the five-year period that will show the net advantage or disadvantage of purchasing the automatic dryer. Ignore income taxes, and use only relevant costs in your analysis.

Cost of new machine	($ 8,000)
Savings in operating costs ($4,500 - $2,500) 5 years	20,000
Salvage value of old machine	4,000
	$ 2,000

The laundry department will be $2,000 better off if the new machine is purchased.

Solution – Exercise 6 – 2 Golden Years Inc. operates three retirement facilities and expects the following results for the coming year.

	The Oaks	The Pines	The Elms	Total
Revenue	$100,000	$150,000	$180,000	$430,000
Variable costs	45,000	60,000	60,000	165,000
Contribution margin	55,000	90,000	120,000	265,000
Fixed costs	80,000	50,000	60,000	190,000
Net income (loss)	($ 25,000)	$ 40,000	$ 60,000	$ 75,000

Answer each of the following questions independently.

1. Fixed costs are all allocated and unavoidable. What will happen to profit if Golden Yea[r] discontinues operations at The Oaks?

    The profit of Golden Years will be $55,000 less if the operations are discontinued at The Oak[s]. Golden Years would be giving up $55,000 of contribution, but no fixed costs.

2. Suppose now that $25,000 of the fixed costs shown for the Oaks are avoidable. What will happen [to] total profits if Golden Years discontinues operations at The Oaks?

    The profit of Golden Years will be $30,000 less if the operations are discontinued at The Oak[s]. Golden Years would be giving up $55,000 of contribution and only $25,000 of fixed costs.

Solution – Exercise 6 – 3 Joe College graduated from a university that is located three hours from the city in which he now works. A loyal alumnus and an avid football fan, Joe always buys season tickets to the football games although his Alma Mater has posted loosing records in each of the last three years. Joe sends a check for $218 to the University by July 1 of every year to cover the cost of two tickets for each of the 7 home games plus $50 for a parking permit. Joe has difficulty finding friends to accompany him to the games. However, he is adamant that he must go to the games because he has paid for the tickets. Friends insist that the cost of the tickets is a sunk cost and that the decision should be based on future costs that would be different between alternatives – going to the game and not going to the game. In addition, Joe's friends have calculated the fuel for the 6 hour round trip costs $15.00 and two means while away from home for the game can easily cost $30 or more. Write a memo to Joe outlining the relevant costs associated with a trip to the game.

Dear Joe,

    As a friend I must advise you to analyze the cost of attending the games at your alma mater. The season tickets are purchased and paid for early in July. Therefore, at the time the first football game is played, the cost of the season tickets is considered a sunk cost and would not be considered a relevant cost.   Also, you must consider the cost of the gasoline and the additional cost of eating two means away from home. Hopefully, the information provided in this memo will be beneficial to you.

Your friend

Solution – Problem 6 – 4

Chip Drayer has just inherited a peanut farm from his father. Chip estimates that he can produce 10,000 pounds of peanuts for approximately $12,500. Chip can sell the peanuts as they come from the field for $2.00 per pound. Alternatively, Chip can have the peanuts processed further at a cost of $0.15 per pound and sell them as roasted peanuts for $2.50.

1. Define joint cost.

    The cost of common inputs when two or more products are produced simultaneously

2. What is the joint cost associated with producing the peanuts?

    $12,500, the cost of producing the peanuts

3. Define split-off point.

    The stage of production at which individual products are identifiable

4.   Should Chip sell the peanuts for $2.00 as they come from the field or process the peanuts further and sell them at $2.50 as roasted peanuts? Provide figures to support your conclusion.

    Chip should process the peanuts further and sell them at $2.50 per pound as roasted peanuts. The relevant cost to consider are the selling costs at the split-off point and after further processing - $2.50 per pound - $2.00 per pound = $.50 per pound. To process the peanuts further only costs $ .15. Comparing the additional revenue of $ .50 per pound to the additional cost $ .15 per pound, Chip would better off by $ .35 per pound to process the peanuts further and sell them as roasted peanuts.

Solution – Problem 6 – 5

Paz makes an electric skateboard-like scooter that is small enough to fit into a school locker. Production for the year 2004 is budgeted at 20,000 scooters. Currently, Paz makes all of the parts for manufacturing the scooter. However, an outside source has offered to make and sell Paz 20,000 steering columns for $90 each. The controller of Paz has researched the cost to produce the steering column in house and has found the following cost structure:

Variable costs –	
Direct materials	$48
Direct labor	23
Overhead	16
Total variable cost per unit	87

Fixed costs of $40,000 represents depreciation on special equipment designed to make the steering columns. The equipment cannot be used for any other purpose. The supervisory salary of $50,000 is for the supervisor of the assembly line where the steering columns are made. The supervisor is not involved with the manufacture of any other parts. Therefore, his salary can be eliminated if the steering columns are purchased. The other fixed costs are allocated costs and cannot be eliminated. Help the controller evaluate the offer to purchase the steering columns by completing the schedules below.

Incremental Cost Analysis
Paz Company
Make or Buy Decision

	Cost of Manufacturing 20,000 Units	Cost of Buying 20,000 Units	Incremental Cost (Savings)
Variable costs			
Direct material	960,000	$ -0-	$(960,000)
Direct labor	460,000		(460,000)
Variable overhead	320,000	-0-	(320,000)
Total variable costs	$1,740,000	$ -0-	($1,740,000)
Fixed Costs			
Depreciation	$40,000	$40,000	-0-
Supervisory salaries	50,000		(50,000)
Other	2,000	2,000	-0-
Total fixed costs	82,000	42,000	(50,000)
Cost of buying units	-0-	$1,800,000	$1,800,000
Total	$1,832,000	$1,842,000	$ 10,000

Incremental Cost Analysis
Company

Cost of buying		
(20,000 units @ $90)		$1,800,000
Cost savings (avoidable if purchase units outside):		
Variable costs	$1,740,000	
Other	50,000	1,790,000
Excess cost of buying units from outside vender		$ 10,000

CHAPTER 7

Capital Budgeting Decisions

CHAPTER INTRODUCTION

This chapter, involving problems relating to capital budgeting decisions, extends the discussion of decision making from Chapter 6. The chapter discusses how to determine whether future cash inflows are sufficient to earn a satisfactory return.

Objectives, Terms, and Discussions

LO1   *Define capital expenditure decisions and capital budgets.*

Investment decisions involving the acquisition of long-lived assets are often referred to as **capital expenditure decisions** (also referred to as **capital budgeting decisions**) because they require that capital (company funds) be expended to acquire additional resources. The process of evaluating the investment opportunities is referred to as capital budgeting, and the final list of approved projects is referred to as the **capital budget**.

Crucial to an understanding of capital budgeting decisions is an understanding of the time value of money. The time value of money concept recognizes that it is better to receive a dollar today than it is to receive a dollar next year or any other time in the future. This is because the dollar received today can be invested so that at the end of the year it amounts to more than a dollar. To simplify present value calculations, managers can use present value tables to look up present value factors. Present value tables are found in Appendix C of the textbook.

LO2   *Evaluate investment opportunities using the net present value approach.*

The time value of money forms the basis of the net present value method for evaluating capital investments. The net present value method consists of three steps:

- Identify amount and period for investment
- Determine net present value of cash flows
- Evaluate the net present value

The first step is to identify the amount and time period of each cash flow associated with the potential investment. The cash flows may be positive (inflows of cash) or negative (outflows of cash). The only relevant cash flows are those that are incremental (those that increase or decrease if a decision alternative is selected). The second step is to equate or discount the cash flows to their present values using a required rate of return. Assume the **required rate of return** (also called the hurdle rate) is the minimum return that top management wants to earn on investments. The third and final step is to evaluate the net present value. The sum of the present values of all cash flows (inflows and outflows) is the **net present value (NPV)** of the investment. If the NPV is zero, the investment is generating a rate of return exactly equal to the required rate of return. If the NPV is zero or positive, the investment should be undertaken. Investment opportunities that have a negative NPV are generally not acceptable. A comprehensive example of the NPV approach is given in the text.

LO3   *Evaluate investment opportunities using the internal rate of return approach.*

Like the NPV, the internal rate of return method takes into account the time value of money. The **internal rate of return (IRR)** is the rate of return that equates the present value of future cash flows to the investment outlay. If the IRR of a potential investment is equal to or greater than the required rate of return, the investment should be undertaken. In performing present value analysis in previous examples, an annuity was multiplied by a present value factor to find the present value. For calculating the IRR, set the present value equal to the initial outlay for the investment. Then solve for the present value factor and use it to look up the rate of return implicit in the investment. An example of the IRR is presented in the text.

$$\text{Present value factor} = \frac{\text{Initial outlay}}{\text{Annuity amount}}$$

In practice, the required rate of return must be estimated by management. Under certain conditions, the required rate of return should be equal to the cost of capital for the firm. The **cost of capital** is the weighted average of the costs of debt and equity financing used to generate capital for investments.

The NPV method and the IRR method are similar in that they both consider the time value of money. However, they differ in the evaluation of investment alternatives. The NPV method leads to accepting an investment alternative with a zero or positive NPV while the IRR requires the IRR to be greater than a required return before an investment alternative is accepted.

LO4   *Calculate the depreciation tax shield, and explain why depreciation is important in investment analysis only because of income taxes.*

Tax considerations play a major role in capital budgeting decisions. If an investment project generates taxable revenue, cash inflows from the project will be reduced by the taxes that must be paid on the revenue. If an investment project generates tax-deductible expenses, cash inflows from the project will be increased by the tax savings resulting from the decrease in income taxes payable. Although depreciation does not directly affect cash flow, it indirectly affects cash flow because it reduces the amount of tax a company must pay. Depreciation is deducted to arrive at income before taxes and reduces the amount of income taxes that must be paid. **Depreciation tax shield** refers to the tax savings resulting from depreciation.

LO5 *Use the payback period and the accounting rate of return methods to evaluate investment opportunities.*

The net present value and the internal rate of return methods are widely used. However, more simple approaches are also used to evaluate capital projects. Two of these are the payback period method and the accounting rate of return method.

The **payback period** is the length of time it takes to recover the initial cost of an investment. For example, if an investment opportunity cost $1,000, and yields cash inflows of $500 per year, it has a payback period of two years. One approach to using the payback method is to accept investment projects that have a payback period less than some specified requirement. A problem with the payback method is that it does not take into account the total stream of cash flows related to an investment. It only considers the stream of cash flows up to the time the investment is paid back. Another problem is that the payback method does not consider the time value of money.

The **accounting rate of return** is equal to the average after-tax income from a project divided by the average investment in the project.

$$\text{Accounting Rate of Return (ARR)} = \frac{\text{Average Net Income}}{\text{Average Investment}}$$

The accounting rate of return can be used to evaluate investment opportunities by comparing their accounting rates of return with a required accounting rate of return. A limitation of this approach is that it ignores the time value of money.

LO6 *Explain why managers may concentrate erroneously on the short-run profitability of investments rather than their net present value.*

Managers who wish to maximize shareholder wealth should use present value techniques to evaluate investments. However, managers may be discouraged from using present value techniques because of the way in which their own performance is evaluated. If a manager knows that job performance is evaluated in terms of reported accounting income, he or she may fear being fired because of the low initial profits of the investment resulting from high amounts of depreciation in early years and low revenue in early start-up years. A partial solution to this problem is to make sure managers realize that, if they approve projects with positive net present values that lower reported income in the short run, evaluations of their performance and their compensation will take the expected future benefits into account.

LOA1 *Explain how the IRR is calculated when there are uneven cash flows.*

For cases where the cash flows are not equal, the IRR approach discussed previously cannot be used because we cannot divide the initial investment by a single cash flow annuity to yield a present value factor. Instead, we must estimate the IRR and use the estimate to calculate the net present value of the project. If the net present value is greater than zero, the estimate of the IRR should be increased. If the net present value is less than zero, the estimate should be decreased. By estimating the IRR in this trial-and-error fashion, it is possible to eventually arrive a the actual rate of return. Computer spreadsheet programs and some pocket calculators contain functions that easily estimate the IRR of a project.

LOB1 *Discuss criticisms of time value of money approaches to evaluating investment opportunities.*

The time value of money approaches discussed in this chapter are subject to a number of criticisms. Most of the criticisms relate more to inappropriate use of NPV or IRR than to some inherent flaw in the methods. Critics contend that these methods may lead companies to underinvest.

Critics have concluded that firms tend to use excessively high required rates of return, leading to negative net present values and rejection of sound investment opportunities. Some managers believe that they must set the rates high to counter subordinates' overly optimistic projections of cash flow when they want their projects funded. Other managers believe that high required rates motivate subordinates to work especially hard to search out investments with exceptional promise.

Time value of money approaches require that managers specify all cash inflows and outflows of potential investments. However, there seems to be a tendency for managers to ignore cash inflows that are far in the future because these cash inflows are highly uncertain. Ignoring these cash inflows entirely clearly understates their value, leading to underinvestment in suitable projects. Ignoring cash flows that are far in the future is simply an error in applying time value of money techniques.

One of the most significant problems in applying time value of money approaches is that so-called soft benefits are often not taken into account because these soft benefits are difficult to quantify in dollar terms. For example, a manager may fail to consider that a project may improve the firm's reputation as an industry leader or that a project may be a source of competitive advantage. Ignoring soft benefits may lead firms to pass up investments that are of strategic importance. Managers should make a reasonable effort to calculate the cash value of soft benefits when analyzing investment opportunities.

Review of Key Terms

Accounting rate of return: The average after-tax income from a project divided by the average investment.

Capital budget: The list of approved capital expenditures developed after an analysis of potential projects.

Capital budgeting decision: Investment decision involving the acquisition of long-lived assets.

Capital expenditure decision: Investment decision involving the acquisition of long-lived assets.

Cost of capital: The weighted average of the costs of debt and equity financing used to generate capital for investments.

Depreciation tax shield: The tax savings resulting from depreciation.

Internal rate of return: The rate of return that equates the present value of future cash flows to the investment outlay.

Net present value: The sum of the present values of all cash flows (alternatively, the present value of future cash inflows less the cost of an investment).

Payback period: The length of time it takes to recover the initial cost of an investment.

Present value analysis: A method of investment analysis that expresses future cash flows in terms of their value today.

Required rate of return: The minimum acceptable return on an investment; also referred to as a hurdle rate.

Chapter 7 – True/False

_____ 1. The time value of money concept recognizes that it is not always better to receive a dollar today than it is to receive a dollar at another time in the future.

_____ 2. An advantage of using the accounting rate of return approach is that it considers the time value of money.

_____ 3. Managers who wish to maximize shareholder wealth should use present value techniques to evaluate investments.

_____ 4. Investment decisions involving the acquisition of long-lived assets are referred to as capital budgeting expenditures because they require that capital (company funds) be expended to acquire additional resources.

_____ 5. In using the net present value approach, the NPV must be positive for the investment to be undertaken.

_____ 6. If the IRR of a potential investment is equal to or greater than the required return rate, the investment should be undertaken.

_____ 7. Tax considerations do not play a role in capital budgeting decisions.

_____ 8. A company can use the accounting rate of return to evaluate an investment opportunity by comparing its accounting rate of return to its internal rate of return.

_____ 9. The time value of money forms the basis of the net present value method for evaluating capital investments.

_____ 10. The required rate of return is also called the capital rate.

_____ 11. Most of the criticisms of time value of money approaches relate more to inappropriate use of NPV or IRR than to some inherent flaw in the methods.

_____ 12. Ignoring soft benefits will not lead firms to pass up investments that are of strategic importance.

Chapter 7 – Key Terms Matching

Match the terms, found in Chapter 7, with the following definitions:

a.   accounting rate of return
b.   capital budget
c.   capital budgeting decision
d.   capital expenditure decision
e.   cost of capital
f.   depreciation tax shield

g.   internal rate of return
h.   net present value
i.   required rate of return
j.   payback period
k.   present value analysis

_____   1.   The sum of the present values of all cash flows (alternatively, the present value of future cash inflows less the cost of an investment).

_____   2.   The weighted average of the costs of debt and equity financing used to generate capital for investments.

_____   3.   The length of time it takes to recover the initial cost of an investment.

_____   4.   The average after-tax income from a project divided by the average investment.

_____   5.   The rate of return that equates the present value of future cash flows to the investment outlay.

_____   6.   The list of approved capital expenditures developed after an analysis of potential projects.

_____   7.   Investment decision involving the acquisition of long-lived assets.

_____   8.   A method of investment analysis that expresses future cash flows in term of their value today.

_____   9.   The minimum acceptable return on an investment

_____   10.   The tax savings resulting from depreciation.

Chapter 7 – Multiple Choice

1.   In evaluating an investment opportunity, a company must know
    a.   how much cash it receives from or pays for an investment.
    b.   when the cash is to be received or paid.
    c.   both a and b.
    d.   none of the above.

2.   The techniques developed to equate future dollars to current dollars are referred to as
    a.   present value techniques or time value of money methods.
    b.   present value techniques or opportunity cost analysis.
    c.   time value of money methods or opportunity cost analysis.
    d.   none of the above.

3.   If you wish to have $10,000 at the end of four years, what amount must you invest today if your investment earns an annual interest rate of 12 percent each year?
    a. $7,118
    b. $3,037
    c. $6,355
    d.   none of the above

4.   Which of the following methods take into consideration the concept of time value of money?
    a.   Internal rate of return
    b.   Payback period method
    c.   Accounting rate of return
    d.   All of the above use the time value of money concept

5.   The cost of equity is
    a.   the interest that is incurred and must be paid to creditors.
    b.   the values of benefits foregone by selecting one investment over another.
    c.   stockholders' equity divided by total assets.
    d.   the return demanded by stockholders for the risk they bear in supplying capital.

6.   Payback period equals
    a.   initial cost of an investment divided by present value of net cash flows.
    b.   initial cost of an investment divided by net annual cash flows.
    c.   net cash flows divided by initial cost of an investment.
    d.   initial cost of an investment divided by a specified number of years.

7.   A major limitation of the payback period method is
    a.   it ignores the time value of money.
    b.   it ignores all cash flows that occur after the investment is paid back.
    c.   both a and b.
    d.   neither a nor b.

8.   The net present value method requires a proper specification of cash flows. Which of the following costs would not be considered an outflow of cash?
    a.   Direct labor cost
    b.   Price paid for equipment
    c.   Taxes
    d.   Depreciation

9.   The Pet Beauty Emporium is considering the purchase of a machine to improve the quality and efficiency of its grooming service. The new machine is expected to generate an additional $5,000 in annual revenue. The machine will cost $32,000 and will have a useful life of 10 years. The internal rate of return on the machine is
    a.   6.4%.
    b.   9%.
    c.   15.6%.
    d.   20%.

10.   The accounting rate of return is equal to
    a.   average net income divided by average investment.
    b.   average sales divided by average investment.
    c.   average net income divided by average sales.
    d.   average sales divided by average net income.

11.   Quarters Inn is a boarding stable for horses. The company has purchased a machine that will automatically drop hay into stalls periodically. The machine cost $50,000, but will save $8,000 each year in labor other operating costs. The machine has an expected useful life of 15 years with no salvage value. The payback period on the machine will be
    a.   6.25 years.
    b.   2.4 years.
    c.   15 years.
    d.   none of the above.

12.   Which of the following is not a criticism of time value of money approaches to evaluating investments?
    a.   Excessively high required rates of return discourage investment
    b.   Ignoring cash inflows far in the future discourages investment
    c.   Failure to consider soft benefits discourages investment
    d.   All of the above are criticisms of time value of money approaches.

Exercise 7 – 1 Jerry has just won the grand prize in the Powerball lottery. Jerry has the option of receiving $30,000,000 immediately **or** receiving 4,000,000 each year for ten years at which time he will receive a lump sum of $10,000,000. Assuming you are Jerry's financial advisor and that you can invest money at a 10 percent rate of return, which option will you suggest he choose? Show computations to support your answer.

Exercise 7 – 2 Your grandmother has offered to give you money for an investment provided you can choose the best investment alternative. Listed below is information concerning the cash flows of Investment A and Investment B, both of which earn an annual interest rate of 12% and require the same initial investment.

	Investment A	Investment B
Year 1	$ 1,000	$5,000
2	2,000	4,000
3	3,000	3,000
4	4,000	2,000
5	5,000	1,000
	$15,000	$15,000

1. Which investment alternative will you choose?

2. Why is your investment choice worth more than the alternative choice?

Exercise 7 – 3   Robert and Jennifer have three children ages 6, 8 and 12. They want to have at least $40,000 set aside for each of them when they reach college age. Assuming interest rates of 10%, how much would they have to invest for each child today to have $40,000 when they reach 18?

6-year old _____

8-year old _____

12-year old _____

Problem 7 – 4   As you may recall from Exercise 6 – 4, Chip Drayer operates a peanut farm. Chip is considering purchasing a machine that will dip the peanuts in milk chocolate. The machine would cost $120,000. Chip has determined that the new machine would increase the company's annual net cash inflows by approximately $21,200. The machine would have a 12-year useful life and no salvage value.

1.   Calculate the pay-back period.

2.   Calculate machine's the internal rate of return.

3.   Calculate the machine's net present value using a discount rate of 10%.

4.   Assuming Chip's cost of capital is 10%, is the investment acceptable? Why or why not?

Problem 7 – 5   Will Wash has gained valuable experience as manager of the laundry department at the Hooty Snooty Hotel and is considering going into the laundry business. The construction of a building and the purchase of necessary laundry equipment are estimated to cost $1,260,000. Both the building and equipment will be depreciated over 12 years using the straight-line method. The building and equipment are expected to have zero salvage values at the end of the 12 years. Will's required rate of return for this project is 13%. Estimated annual net income and cash flows related to the laundry are as follows:

Revenue	$658,000
Less:	
Utility cost	80,000
Supplies	16,000
Labor	252,000
Depreciation	105,000
Other	9,000
Income before taxes	$196,000
Taxes at 40%	78,400
Net income	$117,600

1.   What is the net present value of the investment in the laundry?

2.   Calculate the internal rate of return of the investment.

3.   Calculate the payback period of the investment.

Solutions – Chapter 7 – True/False

1. F The time value of money concept recognizes that it is always better to receive a dollar today than it is to receive a dollar at another time in the future.
2. F The primary limitation of using the accounting rate of return method is that, like the payback period method, it ignores the time value of money.
3. T
4. T
5. F In using the net present value approach the NPV must be zero or positive for the investment to be undertaken.
6. T
7. F Tax considerations play a major role in capital budgeting decisions.
8. F A company can use the accounting rate of return to evaluate an investment opportunity by comparing its accounting rate of return to its required rate of return.
9. T
10. F The required rate of return is also called the hurdle rate.
11. T
12. F Ignoring soft benefits may lead firms to pass up investments that are of strategic importance.

Solutions – Chapter 7 – Key Terms Matching

1.   h. net present value
2.   e. cost of capital
3.   j. payback period
4.   a. accounting rate of return
5.   g. internal rate of return
6.   b. capital budget

7.   d or c capital budgeting decision or capital expenditure decision
8.   k. present value analysis
9.   i. required rate of return
10.   f. depreciation tax shield

Solutions – Chapter 7 – Multiple Choice

1. c
2. a
3. c
4. a
5. d
6. b

7. c
8. d
9. b
10. a
11. a
12. d

Solution − Exercise 7 − 1   Jerry has just won the grand prize in the Powerball lottery. Jerry has the option of receiving $30,000,000 immediately **or** receiving 4,000,000 each year for ten years at which time he will receive a lump sum of $10,000,000. Assuming you are Jerry's financial advisor and that you can invest money at a 10 percent rate of return, which option will you suggest he choose? Show computations to support your answer.

Jerry should take the $30,000,000 immediately. That option has a present value of $30,000,000. The other option is worth $28,433,400 calculated as follows:

$ 4,000,000
<u>× 6.1446</u>   (factor for present value of an annuity of $1, 10 years, interest rate 10%)
<u>$24,578,400</u>

$10,000,000
<u>× .3855</u>   (factor for present value of $1, 10 years, interest rate 10%)
<u>$ 3,855,000</u>

The total of the two income streams is:

$24,578,400
<u>$ 3,855,000</u>
<u>$28,433,400</u>

Solution − Exercise 7 − 2   Your grandmother has offered to give you money for an investment provided you can choose the best investment alternative. Listed below is information concerning the cash flows of Investment A and Investment B, both of which earn an annual interest rate of 12% and require the same initial investment.

	Investment A	Factor 12%	NPV	Investment B	Factor 12%	NPV
Year 1	$ 1,000	× 0.8929 =	$ 892.90	$ 5,000	× 0.8929 =	$ 4,464.50
2	2,000	× 0.7972 =	1,594.40	4,000	× 0.7972 =	3,188.80
3	3,000	× 0.7118 =	2,135.40	3,000	× 0.7118 =	2,135.40
4	4,000	× 0.6355 =	2,542.00	2,000	× 0.6355 =	1,271.00
5	<u>5,000</u>	× 0.5674 =	<u>2,837.00</u>	<u>1,000</u>	× 0.5674 =	<u>567.40</u>
	<u>$15,000</u>		<u>$10,001.70</u>	<u>$15,000</u>		<u>$11,627.10</u>

1.   Which investment alternative will you choose and why?

Investment B because the net present value of Investment B is more than the net present value of Investment A by $1,625.40.

2.   Why is your investment choice worth more than the alternative choice?

Investment B is worth more because the cash flows are larger in the early years.

Solution – Exercise 7 – 3   Robert and Jennifer have three children ages 6, 8 and 12. They want to have at least $40,000 set aside for each of them when they reach college age. Assuming interest rates of 10%, how much would they have to invest for each child today to have $40,000 when they reach 18?

6-year old $12,744   18 – 6 = 12 years – factor – 0.3186 × $40,000 = $12,744

8-year old $15,420   18 – 8 = 10 years – factor – 0 .3885 × $40,000 = $15,420

12-year old $22,580   18 – 12 = 6 years – factor – 0.5645 × 40,000 = $22,580

Solution – Problem 7 – 4   As you may recall from Exercise 6 – 4, Chip Drayer operates a peanut farm. Chip is considering purchasing a machine that will dip the peanuts in milk chocolate. The machine would cost $120,000. Chip has determined that the new machine would increase the company's annual net cash inflows by approximately $21,200. The machine would have a 12-year useful life and no salvage value.

1.   Calculate the pay-back period.

      $120,000 ÷ $21,200 = 5.6603 years

2.   Calculate machine's the internal rate of return.

      $120,000 ÷ $21,200 = 5.6603 scanning 12 year line , a factor of 5.6603 represents an IRR of 14%.

3.   Calculate the machine's net present value using a discount rate of 10%.

Time Period	Cash Flow	PV Factor	Present Value
- 0 -	($120,000)	1.0000	($120,000)
1 – 12	21,200	6.8137	144,450
		Net present value	$ 24,450

4.   Assuming Chip's cost of capital is 10%, is the investment acceptable? Why or why not?

      Yes. Indications are the investment will earn a return greater than 10%. The internal rate of return is estimated to be 14%. Using the factor for 10%, the net present value is positive.

Solution – Problem 7 – 5 Will Wash has gained valuable experience as manager of the laundry department at the Hooty Snooty Hotel and is considering going into the laundry business. The construction of a building and the purchase of necessary laundry equipment are estimated to cost $1,260,000. Both the building and equipment will be depreciated over 12 years using the straight-line method. The building and equipment are expected to have zero salvage values at the end of the 12 years. Will's required rate of return for this project is 13%. Estimated annual net income and cash flows related to the laundry are as follows:

Revenue	$658,000
Less:	
Utility cost	80,000
Supplies	16,000
Labor	252,000
Depreciation	105,000
Other	9,000
Income before taxes	$196,000
Taxes at 40%	78,400
Net income	$117,600

1.   What is the net present value of the investment in the laundry?

		Present Value		
Item		**Cash Flow**	**Factor**	**Present Value**
Initial Investment		($1,260,000)	1.000	($1,260,000)
Revenue	$658,000			
Expense (other than depreciation)	(357,000)			
Taxes	(78,400)	222,600	5.9176	1,317,258
Net present value				$ 57,258

2.   Calculate the internal rate of return of the investment.

$1,260,000 ÷ $ 222,600 = 5.6603, scanning the 12 year line, a factor of 5.6603 represents an IRR of 14%.

3.   Calculate the payback period of the investment.

1,260,000 ÷ $ 222,600 = 5.6603 years

CHAPTER **8**

Budgetary Planning and Control

CHAPTER INTRODUCTION

In business, **budgets** are the formal documents that quantify a company's plans for achieving its goals. The entire planning and control process of many companies is built around budgets. This chapter illustrates the preparation of several budgets that are in common use. It describes the role of budgets in the performance evaluation process and discusses a number of issues associated with budgets.

Objectives, Terms, and Discussions

LO1   *Discuss the use of budgets in planning and control.*

The entire planning and control process of many companies is built around budgets. Budgets are essential for planning and control in various departments, divisions, and companies as a whole.

Budgets are useful in the planning process because they enhance communication and coordination. Developing budgets force managers to consider carefully their goals and objectives and to specify means of achieving them. Budgets communicate information about where the company is heading and aid coordination of managers' activities. For example, the marketing manager may prepare a sales budget, which is, in turn, used by the production manager to aid in material requisitions and scheduling workers.

Budgets are useful in the control process because they provide a basis for evaluating performance. To control a company—to make sure it is heading in the proper direction and operating efficiently—is essential to assess the performance of managers and the operations for which they are responsible. Performance is often evaluated by comparing actual performance with budgeted performance. Significant deviations from planned performance are associated with three potential causes:

- It is possible that the plan or budget was poorly conceived. If a budget is not carefully developed, it should not be surprising that actual results are different from planned results.

- It is possible that although the budget was carefully developed, conditions have changed. For example, if the economy has taken a sudden downturn, actual sales might be less than budgeted sales.
- It is possible that managers have done a particularly good or poor job managing operations. "You get what you measure" is an idea central to the understanding of the control process. If managers know that their performance will be evaluated with respect to the budget, they are likely to work especially hard to achieve budgeted goals.

Often, the group within a company that is responsible for approval of the various budgets is the **budget committee**. The committee generally consists of senior managers, including the president, the chief financial officer, the vice-president for operations, and the controller. The budget committee should work with departments to develop realistic plans that are consistent with overall company goals. The extent to which departments are consulted relates to the distinction between top-down and bottom-up approaches to budget development. In a top-down approach, budgets are developed at higher organizational levels without substantial input from lower level managers. In a bottom-up approach, lower level managers are the primary source of information used in setting the budget. Most managers believe that a successful budgeting process requires a bottom-up approach.

Before a budget can be prepared, managers must decide on an appropriate budget period. In some cases, long-run budgets are prepared for a 5-year or even a 10-year period. In other cases, short-run budgets may cover a month, a quarter, or a year. Generally, the longer the time period, the less detailed the budget.

A common starting point in developing a budget is a consideration of the costs and revenues of the prior period. These amounts may be adjusted up or down based on current information and assumptions of what will happen in the future. **Zero-base budgeting** is another method of budget preparation that requires budgeted amounts to be justified by each department at the start of each budget period. Managers must start from zero in developing their budgets, resulting in a fresh consideration of the validity of budget amounts. However, this technique is time-consuming and expensive and it is not widely used by business enterprises.

LO2 *Prepare the budget schedules that make up the master budget.*

The **master budget** is a comprehensive planning document that incorporates a number of individual budgets. Typically, the master budget includes budgets for sales, production, direct materials, direct labor, manufacturing overhead, selling and administrative expenses, capital acquisitions, and cash receipts and disbursements, as well as a budgeted income statement and a budgeted balance sheet. Many of these budgets are interrelated. For instance, the sales budget influences the production budget, the selling and administrative expenses budget, the cash receipts and disbursements budget, and the budgeted income statement. The production budget figures are needed to complete the direct material purchases budget, the direct labor budget, the manufacturing overhead budget, the cash receipts and disbursements budget, the budgeted income statement, and the budgeted balance sheet.

The first step in the budget process is to develop the sales budget. This budget is prepared first because other budgets cannot be prepared without an estimate of sales. Numerous methods may be used to estimate sales. Large companies may hire economists to prepare sales forecasts using sophisticated mathematical models. Smaller companies may develop budgets based on an analysis of the trend in their own sales data. Other sources of information include trade journals, sales personnel, and professional judgement of managers.

The production budget can be developed after the sales budget is prepared. In deciding how much to produce, managers must take into consideration how much they expect to sell, how much is in beginning inventory, and how much they desire to have in ending inventory. The quantity that must be produced can be calculated from the following formula.

$$
\begin{array}{ccccccc}
\text{Finished} & & \text{Expected} & & \text{Desired ending} & & \text{Beginning} \\
\text{units to be} & = & \text{sales in} & + & \text{inventory of} & - & \text{inventory of} \\
\text{produced} & & \text{units} & & \text{finished units} & & \text{finished units}
\end{array}
$$

The amount of direct materials that must be purchased depends on the amount needed for production, the amount needed for ending inventory, and the amount already in beginning inventory. The amount that must be purchased can be calculated from the following formula.

$$
\begin{array}{ccccccc}
\text{Required} & & \text{Amount} & & \text{Desired ending} & & \text{Beginning} \\
\text{purchases of} & = & \text{required for} & + & \text{inventory of} & - & \text{inventory of} \\
\text{direct materials} & & \text{production} & & \text{direct materials} & & \text{direct materials}
\end{array}
$$

The direct labor budget presents estimated direct labor costs for the period. Direct labor is calculated by multiplying the number of units produced each period by the labor hours per unit and the rate per hour.

The manufacturing overhead budget presents the variable and fixed manufacturing overhead costs. Budget information is also presented for selling and administrative expenses.

Much of the information contained in the previous budgets is utilized in the preparation of the **budgeted income statement**. The sales figure comes from the sales budget. Cost of goods sold requires a calculation of the unit cost of production. The direct material budget, direct labor budget, manufacturing overhead budget, and selling and administrative expense budget information is also used to prepare the budgeted income statement.

The budget for capital assets is referred to as the **capital acquisitions budget**. Acquisitions of capital assets should be carefully planned because they may substantially reduce cash reserves.

In the cash receipts and disbursements budget, managers plan the amount and timing of cash flows. By planning cash receipts and disbursements, companies can anticipate cash shortages and arrange to borrow funds to enhance their cash positions. If cash surpluses are anticipated, companies can seek investment opportunities. To prepare an estimate of cash collections, managers must determine the percent of credit sales revenue that is collected in the period of sale and the percent collected in subsequent periods. To prepare an estimate of cash disbursements, managers must determine the percent of material purchases that is paid in the period of purchase and the percent that is paid in subsequent periods. Managers must determine all other collections and disbursements anticipated during the period.

The last component of the master budget is the **budgeted balance sheet**. This budget is simply a planned balance sheet. Managers use this budget to assess the effect of their planned decisions on the future financial position of the company.

Budgets facilitate control by providing a standard for evaluation. Differences between budgeted and actual amounts are referred to as **budget variances**, and reports that indicate budget variances are referred to as **performance reports**. If actual costs differ from budgeted costs, management should launch an investigation to determine the cause of the difference.

LO3 *Explain why flexible budgets are needed for performance evaluation.*

In evaluating performance using budgets, care must be taken to make sure that the level of activity used in the budget is equal to the actual level of activity. A **static budget** is not adjusted for the actual level of production. A more appropriate analysis of performance makes use of a **flexible budget**, which is a set of budget relationships that can be adjusted to various activity levels. Flexible budgets take into account the fact that when production increases or decreases, total variable costs change. Total fixed cost, however, stay the same.

Significant deviations from the budget have three major causes: the budget may not have been well conceived, conditions may have changed, or managers' job performance may have been particularly good or bad. The cause of a variance cannot be determined without an investigation. The cost of investigation makes it impractical to investigate all budget variances. A **management by exception** approach is more economical. Using this approach, only exceptional variances— variances that are large in absolute dollars or relative to budgets amount—are investigated. Both "favorable" and "unfavorable" exceptional variances should be investigated.

LO4 *Discuss the conflict between the planning and control uses of budgets.*

Conflict is inherent in the planning and control uses of the budget. Top management would like the managers responsible for carrying out plans to participate in the development of budgets since these managers have the best knowledge of the technology and costs of their operations. However, because their performance is evaluated in comparison to the budget, these mangers have the incentive to make sure that the budget contains some **slack.** That is, they want budgeted goals that are easily achieved.

Historically, budgets have primarily included dollar amounts. However, including some nonmonetary measures of performance in the budget is likely to be advantageous. Because a key aspect of a company's success is high-quality, defect-free products, it may be useful to budget the number of defects and the number of customer complaints to be used to judge performance.

Review of Key Terms

Budget: A formal document that quantifies a company's plan for achieving its goals.

Budget committee: The group responsible for preparing budgets.

Budget variance: The difference between budgeted and actual cost.

Flexible budget: A budget that is adjusted for the actual level of activity.

Management by exception: Policy by which managers investigate departures (or variances) from planned results that appear to be exceptional: they do not investigate minor departures (or variances) from the plan.

Master budget: A comprehensive planning document that incorporates a number of individual budgets.

Slack: Amounts (padding) managers include in budgets to assure that budgeted goals can be easily achieved.

Static budget: A budget that is not adjusted for the actual level of activity.

Zero-base budgeting: A method of budget preparation that requires each department to justify budgeted amounts at the start of each budget period, even if the amounts were supported in prior periods.

Chapter 8 – True/False

_T_   1.   Budgets are useful in the planning process because they enhance communication and coordination.

_T_   2.   Budgets are useful in the control process because they provide a basis for evaluating performance.

_F_   3.   In a top-down approach, budgets are developed at higher organizational levels with substantial input from lower level managers.

_T_   4.   A common starting point in developing a budget is a consideration of the costs and revenues of the prior period.

_F_   5.   A zero-base budgeting technique is simple and widely used by business enterprises.

_F_   6.   The first step in the budget process is to develop the budgeted income statement.

_T_   7.   In deciding how much to produce, managers must take into consideration how much they expect to sell, how much is in beginning inventory, and how much they desire to have in ending inventory.

_F_   8.   In the direct labor budget, direct labor is calculated by multiplying the number of units sold each period by the labor hours per unit and the rate per hour.

_T_   9.   In evaluating performance using budgets, care must be taken to make sure that the budgeted level of activity is equal to the actual level of activity.

_F_   10.   Flexible budgets take into account the fact that when production increases or decreases, total fixed costs change.

_F_   11.   Nonmonetary measures of performance should not be included in budgets.

_T_   12.   Budgets facilitate control by providing a standard for evaluation.

Chapter 8 – Key Terms Matching

Match the terms, found in Chapter 8, with the following definitions:

a. budget
b. budget committee
c. budget variance
d. flexible budget
e. management by exception

f. master budget
g. slack
h. static budget
i. zero-base budgeting

__A__ 1. A formal document that quantifies a company's plan for achieving its goals.

__G__ 2. Amounts (padding) managers include in budgets to assure that budgeted goals can be easily achieved.

__F__ 3. A comprehensive planning document that incorporates a number of individual budgets.

__D__ 4. A budget that is adjusted for the actual level of activity.

__I__ 5. A method of budget preparation that requires each department to justify budgeted amounts at the start of each budget period, even if the amounts were supported in prior periods.

__E__ 6. Policy by which managers investigate departures (or variances) from planned results that appear to be exceptional: they do not investigate minor departures (or variances) from the plan.

__B__ 7. The group responsible for preparing budgets.

__H__ 8. A budget that is not adjusted for the actual level of activity.

__C__ 9. The difference between budgeted and actual costs.

Chapter 8 – Multiple Choice

1.   Deviations from planned performance are associated with which of the following causes?
      a.   The plan or budget was poorly conceived.
      b.   The plan was carefully developed, but the conditions have changed.
      c.   Managers have done a particularly good or poor job managing operations.
      d.   All of the above

2.   Most managers believe that a successful budgeting process requires a
      a.   top-down approach.
      b.   zero-base budgeting process.
      c.   static budget process.
      d.   bottom-up approach.

3.   Which of the following is not a component of the master budget?
      a.   Sales budget
      b.   Production budget
      c.   Performance report
      d.   All of the above are components of the master budget

4.   Which of the following is a method a company may use to estimate sales in the budgeting process?
      a.   Hiring an economist to prepare sales forecasts
      b.   Basing sales on an analysis of the trend in its sales data
      c.   Using professional judgement of managers
      d.   All of the above are methods used to estimate sales

5.   In the production budget, the formula used to calculate finished units to be produced is
      a.   expected sales in units + desired ending inventory – beginning inventory.
      b.   expected sales in units – desired ending inventory + beginning inventory.
      c.   expected sales in dollars + desired ending inventory – beginning inventory.
      d.   expected sales in dollars – desired ending inventory + beginning inventory.

6.   Which of the following budgets is not used in preparing the budgeted income statement?
      a.   Capital acquisitions budget
      b.   Direct material budget
      c.   Production budget
      d.   Selling and administrative expense budget

7.   The figures from the sales budget are needed to complete which of the following budgets?
      a.   Production budget
      b.   Labor budget
      c.   Budgeted cash receipts and disbursements
      d.   All of the above

8.   To prepare an estimate of cash disbursements, managers must determine
      a.   the percent of material purchases that will be paid in subsequent periods.
      b.   the percent of credit sales.
      c.   the dollar amount of anticipated expenditures for the period.
      d.   both a and c.

9. Which of the following is a reason to prepare a budgeted balance sheet?
   a. To assess the cash flows of the company
   b. To assess the effect of planned decisions on the future financial position of the company
   c. To use in the preparation of the capital acquisitions budget
   d. Both a and c

10. Some significant deviations from the budget may not be investigated because
    a. the cost of the investigation may be too high.
    b. the deviations may be too large.
    c. both a and b.
    d. neither a nor b.

11. The major difference in a static budget and a flexible budget is that
    a. a static budget is not adjusted for level of production activity; a flexible budget is adjusted for level of production activity.
    b. a flexible budget is not adjusted for level of production activity; a static budget is adjusted for level of production activity.
    c. a static budget uses total fixed costs; a flexible budget uses fixed cost per unit.
    d. both a and c.

12. In preparing a flexible budget
    a. when production increases or decreases, total variable costs change.
    b. when production increases or decreases, total fixed costs change.
    c. when production increases or decreases, variable costs per unit change.
    d. both a and b.

Exercise 8 – 1 Alpine Slopes, Inc. produces freestyle snowboards designed for use on all mountain terrain. Production for 2004, the first year of operations, was budgeted at 2,000 snowboards. However, sales have far exceeded predictions. Therefore, in preparing the 2005 budget Alpine is projecting sales of 150% of the amount budgeted for 2004. Alpine plans to continue selling the snowboards for $250 each.

1.   Prepare a sales budget for Alpine for the year 2005.

Sales Budget
For the Year Ending December 31, 2005

	First Quarter	Second Quarter	Third Quarter	Fourth Quarter	Year
Prior year sales in units	600	800	400	200	2,000
Projected sales (150% of prior year)	_____	_____	_____	_____	_____
Sales price per unit	$_____	$_____	$_____	$_____	$_____
Budgeted sales revenue	$_____	$_____	$_____	$_____	$_____

2.   Alpine likes to keep an ending inventory equal to 10 percent of next quarter's sales. Sales in the first quarter of 2006 are budgeted to be 1,080 units. On January 1, 2005, there were 90 snowboards in the finished goods inventory. Prepare a production budget for Alpine for 2005.

Production Budget
For the Year Ending December 31, 2005

	First Quarter	Second Quarter	Third Quarter	Fourth Quarter	Year
Unit sales	_____	_____	_____	_____	_____
Plus desired ending inventory of finished units	_____	_____	_____	_____	_____
Total needed	_____	_____	_____	_____	_____
Less beginning inventory of finished units	_____	_____	_____	_____	_____
Units to be produced	══════	══════	══════	══════	══════

Exercise 8 – 2 The cost of direct materials for one snowboard is estimated to be $80. On January 1, 2005 the balance in raw materials inventory totaled $14,400. Alpine desires to have 20 percent of the next quarter's production needs on hand at the end of each quarter. Alpine plans to produce 1,136 snowboards in the first quarter of 2006. Therefore, the ending inventory in direct materials in the fourth quarter of 2005 should be $18,176.

1.   Prepare a quarterly direct material purchases budget for Alpine for the year 2005.

Direct Material Purchases Budget
For the Year Ending December 31, 2005

	First Quarter	Second Quarter	Third Quarter	Fourth Quarter	Year
Units to be produced	_____	_____	_____	_____	_____
Cost of parts per unit	$_____	$_____	$_____	$_____	$_____
Costs of parts needed	_____	_____	_____	_____	_____
Plus desired ending inventory	_____	_____	_____	_____	_____
Total needed	_____	_____	_____	_____	_____
Less beginning inventory	_____	_____	_____	_____	_____
Cost of purchases	$_____	$_____	$_____	$_____	$_____

2.   The snowboards are hand finished, requiring 12 hours of direct labor for each snowboard. Employees working on the snowboards average $6 per hour and work 480 hours per quarter. Prepare a quarterly direct labor budget for Alpine for 2005.

Direct Labor Budget
For the Year Ending December 31, 2005

	First Quarter	Second Quarter	Third Quarter	Fourth Quarter	Year
Direct labor hours	_____	_____	_____	_____	_____
Labor rate per hour	$_____	$_____	$_____	$_____	$_____
Direct labor cost per unit	_____	_____	_____	_____	_____
Units to be produced	_____	_____	_____	_____	_____
Direct labor cost	$_____	$_____	$_____	$_____	$_____
Total hours	_____	_____	_____	_____	
Hours per quarter per employee	_____	_____	_____	_____	
Number of employees needed	_____	_____	_____	_____	

Exercise 8 – 2 (continued)

3.   Alpine Slopes had the following budgeted overhead for 2005:
        Variable manufacturing overhead –

Indirect materials	$4 per unit
Indirect labor	2 per unit
Other variable costs	1 per unit

        Fixed manufacturing overhead –

Supervisory salaries	$30,000
Depreciation of plant and equipment	10,000 quarters 1, 2, and 3;
	13,000 quarter 4
Other fixed costs	2,000

Prepare a manufacturing overhead budget for Alpine Slopes for the year 2005.

Manufacturing Overhead Budget
For the Year Ending December 31, 2005

	First Quarter	Second Quarter	Third Quarter	Fourth Quarter	Year
Units to be produced					
Variable costs	$	$	$	$	$
Indirect material					
Indirect labor					
Other variable costs					
Total variable overhead					
Fixed costs:					
Supervisory salaries					
Depreciation, plant and equip					
Other fixed costs					
Total fixed overhead					
Total overhead					
Less depreciation					
Cash payments for overhead	$	$	$	$	$

Estimated overhead rate = annual overhead ÷ annual production

$_____ per unit   = $_____   ÷   3,018 units

Exercise 8 – 3 For the year 2005 Alpine has budgeted the following selling and administrative expenses:

Salaries	$50,000
Advertising	40,000
Depreciation of office equipment	2,000 quarters 1 and 2
	2,600 quarters 3 and 4
Other	2,000

1. Using the information presented above, prepare a selling and administrative expense budget for Alpine Slopes for the year ending December 31, 2005.

Selling and Administrative Expense Budget
For the Year Ending December 31, 2005

	First Quarter	Second Quarter	Third Quarter	Fourth Quarter	Year
Salaries	$_____	$_____	$_____	$_____	$_____
Advertising	_____	_____	_____	_____	_____
Depreciation of office equip	_____	_____	_____	_____	_____
Other	_____	_____	_____	_____	_____
Total	$_____	$_____	$_____	$_____	$_____
Less depreciation	_____	_____	_____	_____	_____
Cash disbursements for selling and administrative expense	$_____	$_____	$_____	$_____	$_____

2. Use information found in the budgets prepared in previous exercises to prepare a budgeted income statement for Alpine Slopes for the year ending December 31, 2005.

Budgeted Income Statement
For the Year Ending December 31, 2005

	First Quarter	Second Quarter	Third Quarter	Fourth Quarter	Year
Sales	$_____	$_____	$_____	$_____	$_____
Less cost of goods sold	_____	_____	_____	_____	_____
Gross margin	_____	_____	_____	_____	_____
Less selling and adm expenses	_____	_____	_____	_____	_____
Net income	$_____	$_____	$_____	$_____	$_____

Exercise 8 – 3 (continued)

3. On July 1, 2005 Alpine Slopes bought a new copy machine for $12,000. The machine is expected to have a useful life of 5 years and have no salvage value at the end of its life. In addition, Alpine bought a new sander for finishing the snowboards at a cost of $60,000. The sander was purchased on October 1 and has a useful life of 5 years, after which time it will have a negligible salvage value.

Capital Acquisitions Budget
For the Year Ending December 31, 2005

	First Quarter	Second Quarter	Third Quarter	Fourth Quarter	Year
Office Equipment (5 yr. life)	$_____	$_____	$_____	$_____	$_____
Machinery expense (5 yr. life)	_____	_____	_____	_____	_____
Total	$_____	$_____	$_____	$_____	$_____

Problem 8 − 4 Ten percent of Alpine's sales are cash sales, the remaining 90 percent are credit sales. Sixty percent of the credit sales are collected in the quarter of sale. The remaining 40 percent are collected in the quarter following the sale. All of Alpine's purchases of materials are on credit. Alpine pays for 70 percent of the purchases in the quarter of the purchase while the remaining 30 percent is paid in the subsequent month. Accounts payable as of January 1, 2005 were $8,160. Accounts receivable as of January 1, 2005 were $18,000.

Cash Receipts and Disbursements Budget
For the Year Ending December 31, 2005

	First Quarter	Second Quarter	Third Quarter	Fourth Quarter	Year
Cash receipts	$_____	$_____	$_____	$_____	$_____
Collection of credit sales:					
4th quarter prior year	_____	_____	_____	_____	_____
1st quarter	_____	_____	_____	_____	_____
2nd quarter	_____	_____	_____	_____	_____
3rd quarter	_____	_____	_____	_____	_____
4th quarter	_____	_____	_____	_____	_____
Total cash receipts	_____	_____	_____	_____	_____
Cash disbursements:					
Purchase of materials:					
4th quarter prior year	_____	_____	_____	_____	_____
1st quarter	_____	_____	_____	_____	_____
2nd quarter	_____	_____	_____	_____	_____
3rd quarter	_____	_____	_____	_____	_____
45th quarter	_____	_____	_____	_____	_____
Total purchases disbursements	_____	_____	_____	_____	_____
Payment for direct labor	_____	_____	_____	_____	_____
Payment for mfg. overhead	_____	_____	_____	_____	_____
Payment for selling & admin	_____	_____	_____	_____	_____
Capital acquisitions	_____	_____	_____	_____	_____
Total cash disbursements	_____	_____	_____	_____	_____
Receipts over disbursements	_____	_____	_____	_____	_____
Plus beginning cash balance	_____	_____	_____	_____	_____
Ending cash balance	$_____	$_____	$_____	$_____	$_____

Problem 8 – 5 A balance sheet for Alpine for the year ending December 31, 2004 is presented below. Using information in the 2004 balance sheet and other information contained in the Exercises and Problems in this chapter, prepare a budgeted balance sheet for Alpine as of December 31, 2005.

Balance Sheet
December 31, 2004

Current Assets	
Cash	$ 30,000
Accounts receivable	18,000
Raw material inventory	14,400
Finished goods inventory	19,409
Property, Plant and Equipment (Net)	360,000
Total assets	$441,809
Current Liabilities	
Accounts payable	$ 8,160
Mortgages payable	320,000
Stockholders' Equity	
Common Stock	100,000
Retained Earnings	13,649
Total liabilities and stockholders' equity	$441,809

Budgeted Balance Sheet
December 31, 2005

Current Assets	
Cash	$_____
Accounts receivable	_____
Raw material inventory	_____
Finished goods inventory	_____
Total assets	$_____
Current Liabilities	$_____
Accounts payable	_____
Stockholders' Equity	_____
Common Stock	_____
Retained Earnings	_____
Total liabilities and stockholders' equity	$_____

Solutions – Chapter 8 – True/False

1. T
2. T
3. F   In a top-down approach, budgets are developed at higher organizational levels without substantial input from lower level managers.
4. T
5. F   A zero-base budgeting technique is time-consuming and expensive and it is not widely used by business enterprises.
6. F   The first step in the budget process is to develop the sales budget.
7. T
8. F   In the direct labor budget, direct labor is calculated by multiplying the number of units produced each period by the labor hours per unit and the rate per hour.
9. T
10. F   Flexible budgets take into account the fact that when production increases or decreases, total variable costs change.
11. F   Some nonmonetary measures of performance in the budget is likely to be advantageous.
12. T

Solutions – Chapter 8 – Key Terms Matching

1.	a. budget	6.	e. management by exception
2.	g. slack	7.	b. budget committee
3.	f. master budget	8.	h. static budget
4.	d. flexible budget	9.	c. budget variance
5.	i. zero-base budgeting		

Solutions – Chapter 8 – Multiple Choice

1.	d	7.	d
2.	d	8.	d
3.	c	9.	b
4.	d	10.	a
5.	a	11.	a
6.	a	12.	a

Solution – Exercise 8 – 1

Alpine Slopes, Inc. produces freestyle snowboards designed for use on all mountain terrain. Production for 2004, the first year of operations, was budgeted at 2,000 snowboards. However, sales have far exceeded predictions. Therefore, in preparing the 2005 budget Alpine is projecting sales of 150% of the amount budgeted for 2004. Alpine plans to continue selling the snowboards for $250 each.

1.   Prepare a quarterly sales budget for Alpine for the year 2005.

Sales Budget
For the Year Ending December 31, 2005

	First Quarter	Second Quarter	Third Quarter	Fourth Quarter	Year
Prior year sales in units	600	800	400	200	2000
Projected sales (150% prior year)	900	1200	600	300	3000
Sales price per unit	$250	$250	$250	$250	$250
Budgeted sales revenue	$225,000	$300,000	$150,000	$75,000	$750,000

2.   Alpine likes to keep an ending inventory equal to 10 percent of next quarter's sales. Sales in the first quarter of 2006 are budgeted to be 1,080 units. On January 1, 2005, there were 90 snowboards in the finished goods inventory. Prepare a production budget for Alpine for 2005.

Production Budget
For the Year Ending December 31, 2005

	First Quarter	Second Quarter	Third Quarter	Fourth Quarter	Year
Unit sales	900	1,200	600	300	3,000
Plus desired ending inventory of finished units	120	60	30	108	108
Total needed	1,020	1,260	630	408	3,108
Less beginning inventory of finished units	90	120	60	30	90
Units to be produced	930	1,140	570	378	3,018

Solution – Exercise 8 – 2
The cost of direct materials for one snowboard is estimated to be $80. On January 1, 2005 the balance in raw materials inventory totaled $14,400. Alpine desires to have 20 percent of the next quarter's production needs on hand at the end of each quarter. Alpine plans to produce 1,136 snowboards in the first quarter of 2006. Therefore, the ending inventory in direct materials in the fourth quarter of 2005 should be $18,176.

1.   Prepare a quarterly direct materials purchases budget for Alpine for the year 2005.

Direct Material Purchases Budget
For the Year Ending December 31, 2005

	First Quarter	Second Quarter	Third Quarter	Fourth Quarter	Year
Units to be produced	930	1,140	570	378	3,018
Cost of parts per unit	$ 80	$ 80	$ 80	$ 80	$ 80
Costs of parts needed for production	$74,400	$ 91,200	$45,600	$30,240	$241,440
Plus desired ending inventory of parts	18,240	9,120	6,048	18,176	18,176
Total needed ($)	92,640	100,320	51,648	48,416	259,616
Less beginning inventory of parts	14,400	18,240	9,120	6,048	14,400
Cost of purchases	$78,240	$ 82,080	$42,528	$42,368	$245,216

2.   The snowboards are hand finished, requiring 12 hours of direct labor for each snowboard. Employees working on the snowboards average $6 per hour and work 480 hours per quarter. Prepare a quarterly direct labor budget for Alpine for 2005.

Direct Labor Budget
For the Year Ending December 31, 2005

	First Quarter	Second Quarter	Third Quarter	Fourth Quarter	Year
Direct labor hours	12	12	12	12	12
Labor rate per hour	$ 6	$ 6	$ 6	$ 6	$ 6
Direct labor cost per unit	72	72	72	72	72
Units to be produced	930	1,140	570	378	3,018
Direct labor cost	$66,960	$82,080	$41,040	$27,216	$217,296
Total hours	11,160	13,680	6,840	4,536	
Average hours per quarter per employee	480	80	480	480	
Approximate number of employees needed	24	29	15	10	

Solution – Exercise 8 – 2 Continued

3.   Alpine Slopes had the following budgeted overhead for 2005:

Variable manufacturing overhead –
      Indirect materials $4 per unit
      Indirect labor   2 per unit
      Other variable costs   1 per unit
Fixed manufacturing overhead –
      Supervisory salaries $30,000
      Depreciation of plant and equipment   10,000 quarters 1, 2, and 3;
                                            13,000 quarter 4
      Other fixed costs   2,000

Prepare a manufacturing overhead budget for Alpine Slopes for the year 2005.

Manufacturing Overhead Budget
For the Year Ending December 31, 2005

	First Quarter	Second Quarter	Third Quarter	Fourth Quarter	Year
Units to be produced	930	1,140	570	378	3,018
Variable costs					
Indirect material ($4 per unit)	$ 3,720	$ 4,560	$ 2,280	$ 1,512	$ 12,072
Indirect labor ($2 per unit)	1,860	2,280	1,140	756	6,036
Other variable cost ($1 per unit)	930	1,140	570	378	3,018
Total variable overhead	6,510	7,980	3,990	2,646	21,126
Fixed costs:					
Supervisory salaries	30,000	30,000	30,000	30,000	120,000
Depreciation of plant and equipment	10,000	10,000	10,000	13,000	43,000
Other fixed costs	2,000	2,000	2,000	2,000	8,000
Total fixed overhead	42,000	42,000	42,000	45,000	171,000
Total overhead	$48,510	$49,980	$45,990	$47,646	$192,126
Less depreciation	10,000	10,000	10,000	13,000	43,000
Cash payments for overhead	$38,510	$39,980	$35,990	$34,646	$149,126

Estimated overhead rate = annual overhead ÷ annual production
$192,126 ÷ 3,018 units = $63.66 per unit

Solution – Exercise 8 – 3

For the year 2005 Alpine has budgeted the following selling and administrative expenses:

Salaries	$50,000
Advertising	40,000
Depreciation of office equipment	2,000 quarters 1 and 2
	2,600 quarters 3 and 4
Other	2,000

1. Using the information presented above, prepare a selling and administrative expense budget for Alpine Slopes for the year ending December 31, 2005.

Selling and Administrative Expense Budget
For the Year Ending December 31, 2005

	First Quarter	Second Quarter	Third Quarter	Fourth Quarter	Year
Salaries	$12,500	$12,500	$12,500	$12,500	$50,000
Advertising	10,000	10,000	10,000	10,000	40,000
Depreciation of office equipment	2,000	2,000	2,600	2,600	9,200
Other	500	500	500	500	2,000
Total	25,000	25,000	25,600	25,600	101,200
Less depreciation	2,000	2,000	2,600	2,600	9,200
Cash disbursements for selling and administrative expense	$23,000	$23,000	$23,000	$23,000	$92,000

2. Use information found in the budgets prepared in previous exercises to prepare a budgeted income statement for Alpine Slopes for the year ending December 31, 2005.

Budgeted Income Statement
For the Year Ending December 31, 2005

	First Quarter	Second Quarter	Third Quarter	Fourth Quarter	Year
Sales	$225,000	$300,000	$150,000	$75,000	$750,000
Less cost of goods sold *	194,094	258,792	129,396	64,698	646,980
Gross margin	30,906	41,208	20,604	10,302	103,020
Less selling & admin expenses	25,000	25,000	25,600	25,600	101,200
Net income	$ 5,906	$ 16,208	($ 4,996)	($15,298)	$ 1,820

*Number of units sold @ $215.66 per unit ($80 direct materials, $72 direct labor, $63.66, manufacturing overhead

Solution Exercise 8 – 3 Continued

3.   On July 1, 2005 Alpine Slopes bought a new copy machine for $12,000. The machine is expected to have a useful life of 5 years and have no salvage value at the end of its life. In addition, Alpine bought a new sander for finishing the snowboards at a cost of $60,000. The sander was purchased on October 1 and has a useful life of 5 years, after which time it will have a negligible salvage value.

Capital Acquisitions Budget
For the Year Ending December 31, 2005

	First Quarter	Second Quarter	Third Quarter	Fourth Quarter	Year
Office Equipment (5 yr. life)	- 0 -	- 0 -	$12,000*	- 0 -	$12,000
Machinery expense (5 yr. life)	- 0 -	- 0 -		$60,000**	$60,000**
Total	- 0 -	- 0 -	$12,000	$60,000	$72,000

*   Increases depreciation by 600 in third and fourth quarter ($12,000 ÷5 year life) × ¼ for third and fourth quarter.

**Increases depreciation by $3,000 in fourth quarter ($60,000 ÷5 year life) × ¼ for fourth quarter.

Solution – Problem 8 – 4   Ten percent of Alpine's sales are cash sales, the remaining 90 percent are credit sales. Sixty percent of the credit sales are collected in the quarter of sale. The remaining 40 percent are collected in the quarter following the sale. All of Alpine's purchases of materials are on credit. Alpine pays for 70 percent of the purchases in the quarter of the purchase while the remaining 30 percent is paid in the subsequent month. Accounts payable as of January 1, 2005 were $8,160 and accounts receivable as of January 1, 2005 were $18,000.

Cash Receipts and Disbursements Budget
For the Year Ending December 31, 2005

	First Quarter	Second Quarter	Third Quarter	Fourth Quarter	Year
Cash receipts	$ 22,500	$ 30,000	$ 15,000	$ 7,500	$ 75,000
Collection of credit sales					
4th quarter prior year	18,000				18,000
1st quarter	121,500	81,000			202,500
2nd quarter		162,000	108,000		270,000
3rd quarter			81,000	54,000	135,000
4th quarter				40,500	40,500
Total cash receipts	162,000	273,000	204,000	102,000	741,000
Cash disbursements:					
Purchase of materials:					
4th quarter prior year	$8,160				8,160
1st quarter	54,768	23,472			78,240
2nd quarter		57,456	24,624		82,080
3rd quarter			29,770	12,758	42,528
45th quarter				29,658	29,658
Total cash payments for purchases of materials	62,928	80,928	54,394	42,416	240,666
Payment for direct labor	66,960	82,080	41,040	27,216	217,296
Payment for mfg. overhead	38,510	39,980	35,990	34,646	149,126
Payment for selling & admin.	23,000	23,000	23,000	23,000	92,000
Capital acquisitions			12,000	60,000	72,000
Total cash disbursements	191,398	225,988	166,424	187,278	771,088
Excess of receipts over disbursements	($29,398)	$47,012	$37,576	($85,278)	($30,088)
Plus beginning cash balance	30,000	602	47,614	85,190	30,000
Ending cash balance	$ 602	$47,614	$ 85,190	($ 88)	($ 88)

Solution – Problem 8 – 5

A balance sheet for Alpine for the year ending December 31, 2004 is presented below. Using information in the 2004 balance sheet and other information contained in the Exercises and Problems in this chapter, prepare a budgeted balance sheet for Alpine as of December 31, 2005.

Balance Sheet
December 31, 2004

Current Assets	
Cash	$ 30,000
Accounts receivable	18,000
Raw material inventory	14,400
Finished goods inventory	19,409
Property, Plant and Equipment (Net)	360,000
Total assets	$441,809
Current Liabilities	
Accounts payable	$ 8,160
Mortgages payable	320,000
Stockholders' Equity	
Common Stock	100,000
Retained Earnings	13,649
Total liabilities and stockholders' equity	$441,809

Budgeted Balance Sheet
December 31, 2005

Current Assets	
Cash[a]	($ 88)
Accounts receivable[b]	27,000
Raw material inventory[c]	18,176
Finished goods inventory[d]	23,291
Property plant and equipment (net)[e]	379,800
Total assets	$448,179
Current Liabilities	
Accounts payable[f]	$ 12,710
Mortgage payable	320,000
Stockholders' Equity	
Common Stock	100,000
Retained Earnings[g]	15,469
Total liabilities and stockholders' equity	$448,179

[a]Ending cash balance on Cash Receipts and Disbursements Budget

[b]Cash Receipts and Disbursements Budget 4th quarter sales $75,000 × 90% Credit sales = $67,500 × 40% uncollected = $27,000

[c]Direct Materials Purchases Budget – desired ending inventory - $18,176

[d]Number of snowboards in ending inventory – 108 @ $215.66 = $23,291

[e]Manufacturing Overhead Budget, Selling and Administrative Expense Budget, and Capital Acquisitions Budget $360,000 + purchases $72,000 – depreciation $52,200 = $379,800

[f]Cash Receipts and Disbursements Budget 4th quarter purchases $42,368 × 40%= unpaid amount - $12,710

[g]Balance Sheet, December 31, 2004 $13,649 plus Budgeted Income Statement net income $1,840

CHAPTER **9**

STANDARD COSTS AND VARIANCE ANALYSIS

CHAPTER INTRODUCTION

In a standard costing system, manufactured goods are not recorded at their actual product cost, but rather at the cost that should have been incurred to produce the items. This cost is referred to as standard cost. A primary benefit of a standard costing system is that it allows managers to compare differences between standard and actual costs. These differences are referred to as standard cost variances. Standard costing systems generate variances for direct material, direct labor, and manufacturing overhead. Variance accounts are temporary accounts and are always closed before financial statements are prepared. Standard costs play an important role in controlling operations and determining product costs.

   Standard cost refers to the cost that management believes should be incurred to produce a good or service under anticipated conditions. Some accountants use the terms budgeted cost and standard cost interchangeable. However, the term standard cost often refers to the cost of a single unit, whereas the term budgeted cost refers to the cost, at standard, of the total number of budgeted units.

Objectives, Terms, and Discussions

LO1   *Explain how standard costs are developed.*

Standard costs for material, labor, and manufacturing overhead are developed in a variety of ways. For example, the standard quantity of material may be specified from engineering plans or from recipes or formulas while the standard price may simply be taken from a price list provided by suppliers. The standard quantity of direct labor may be determined by time and motion studies or from an analysis of past data. Standard labor rates are usually set at rates management expects to pay various categories of workers. Developing standard costs for overhead involves procedures similar to the ones used to develop the predetermined overhead rate. Dividing the amount of anticipated overhead by the standard quantity of allocation base results in a standard cost of overhead.

In developing standard costs, some managers emphasize **ideal standards**, and others emphasize **attainable standards**. Ideal standards are developed under the assumption that no obstacles to the production process will be encountered (e.g., machine breakdown, setup time, or raw material defects). Attainable standards are standard costs that do take into account the possibility that a variety of circumstances may lead to costs that are greater than "ideal."

The difference between a standard and an actual cost is referred to as a **standard cost variance**. Companies that have standard costing systems can analyze the standard cost variance, referred to as **variance analysis**, to determine if operations are being performed efficiently. Variance analysis involves separating the difference between standard and actual cost into two components. For direct material the two components are the material price and the material quantity variances. For direct labor the two components are the labor rate and the labor efficiency variances. For manufacturing overhead, the two components are the overhead volume and the controllable overhead variances.

LO2   *Calculate and interpret variances for direct material.*

The **material price variance** is equal to the difference between the actual price per unit of material (AP) and the standard price per unit of material (SP) times the actual quantity of material purchased (AQP).

$$\text{Material price variance} = (AP - SP)\, AQP$$

- Actual prices greater than standard prices are labeled "unfavorable"
- Actual prices less than standard prices are labeled "favorable"

The **material quantity variance** is equal to the difference between the actual quantity of material used (AQU) and the standard quantity of material allowed for the number of units produced (SQ) times the standard price of the material (SP).

$$\text{Material quantity variance} = (AQU - SQ)\, SP$$

- Actual quantities greater than standard quantities allowed for the number of units produced are labeled "unfavorable"
- Actual quantities less than standard quantities allowed for the number of units produced are labeled "favorable"

LO3   *Calculate and interpret variances for direct labor.*

The **labor rate variance** is equal to the difference between the actual wage rate (AR) and the standard wage rate (SR) times the actual number of labor hours worked (AH).

$$\text{Labor rate variance} = (AR - SR)\, AH$$

- Actual rates greater than standard rates are labeled "unfavorable"
- Actual rates less than standard rates are labeled "favorable"

The **labor efficiency variance** is equal to the difference between the actual number of hours worked (AH) and the standard labor hours allowed for the number of units produced (SH) times the standard labor wage rate (SR).

$$\text{Labor efficiency variance} = (AH - SH)\ SR$$

- Actual hours greater than standard hours allowed for the number of units produced are labeled "unfavorable"
- Actual hours less than standard hours allowed for the number of units produced are labeled "favorable"

LO4   *Calculate and interpret variances for manufacturing overhead.*

The total variance for manufacturing overhead is the difference between the overhead applied to inventory at standard rates and actual overhead costs. The total overhead variance can be separated into an overhead volume variance and a controllable overhead variance.

The **controllable overhead variance** is the difference between the actual amount of overhead and the amount of overhead that would be included in a flexible budget for the actual level of production. The variance is "controllable" because managers are expected to be able to control costs so that they are not substantially different from the amount that would be included in the flexible budget.

$$\begin{array}{ccc} \text{Controllable} \\ \text{overhead variance} \end{array} = \text{Actual overhead} - \begin{array}{c}\text{Flexible budget level of}\\ \text{overhead for actual level of}\\ \text{production}\end{array}$$

The **overhead volume variance** is equal to the difference between the amount of overhead included in the flexible budget and the amount of overhead applied to production using the standard overhead rate. The overhead volume variance simply signals that the quantity of production was greater or less than anticipated when the standard overhead rate was developed.

$$\begin{array}{c}\text{Overhead volume}\\ \text{variance}\end{array} = \begin{array}{c}\text{Flexible budget level}\\ \text{of overhead for}\\ \text{actual level of}\\ \text{production}\end{array} - \begin{array}{c}\text{Overhead applied to}\\ \text{production using standard}\\ \text{overhead rate}\end{array}$$

LO5   *Discuss how the management by exception approach is applied to investigation of standard cost variances.*

Most managers take a "management by exception" approach and investigate only those variances that they deem to be exceptional. This implies that some criterion for determining what is meant by "exceptional" must be established. The absolute dollar amount of the variance or the variance as a percent of actual or standard cost is often used at the criterion.

A "favorable" variance does not mean it should not be investigated. For example, the materials price variance may be favorable because cheap, inferior goods are purchased. The purchase of inferior materials may result in a favorable price variance. However, inferior goods may result in scrapped or reworked units or undetected product defects.

LOA1 *Record standard costs in the accounts of a manufacturing firm.*

When a company purchases raw materials, the Raw Material Inventory account is debited for the standard cost of the material purchased. The Accounts Payable account is credited for the actual price. The difference between actual and standard cost is the material price variance. Assume 500 units of raw material are purchased at a cost of $4.50 per unit when the standard price per unit is $5. The appropriate entry is:

Raw Material Inventory	2,500	
Material Price Variance		250
Accounts Payable		2,250

When labor costs are incurred, the Work in Process account is debited for the standard wage rate at the standard number of hours allowed for the units produced. The Wages Payable account is credited for actual wages payable. The difference between actual and standard is included in the labor rate and labor efficiency variance accounts. Assume 10,000 actual labor hours are worked at a rate of $10 per hour. The standard number of hours is 11,000 and the standard wage rate is $12 per hour. The appropriate journal entry is:

Work in Process Inventory	132,000	
Labor Rate Variance		20,000
Labor Efficiency Variance		12,000
Wages Payable		100,000

Recording manufacturing overhead is a three-step process. First, actual overhead is recorded in the Manufacturing Overhead account. Second, overhead is applied to Work in Process at the standard rate. Third, the difference between actual overhead and overhead applied at standard is closed and overhead variances are identified. Assume actual overhead is $80,000 and the overhead applied for 100,000 units is $.75 per unit. The flexible budget amount of overhead for 100,000 units is $70,000. The journal entry to record step one is:

Manufacturing Overhead	80,000	
Various accounts		80,000

The journal entry to record step two is:

Work in Process Inventory	75,000	
Manufacturing Overhead		75,000

The journal entry to record step three is:

Manufacturing Overhead	5,000	($80,000 - $75,000)	
Overhead Volume Variance	5,000	($75,000) - $70,000)	
Controllable Overhead Variance		10,000	($80,000 - $70,000)

When jobs are completed, Work in Process is reduced (credited) and Finished Goods is increased (debited). The appropriate entry is:

Finished Goods	XXX	
Work in Process		XXX

When completed jobs are sold, Finished Goods is reduced (credited) by the cost of the completed jobs and the Cost of Goods Sold account is increased (debited). The appropriate entry is:

Cost of Goods Sold	XXX	
Finished Goods Inventory		XXX

At the end of the accounting period, the temporary variance accounts must be closed. If the variances are not significant, this is usually accomplished by debiting or crediting the variances to Cost of Goods Sold. If the variances are large, the Work in Process, Finished Goods, and Cost of Goods Sold accounts may be allocated portions of the variances.

Review of Key Terms

Attainable standard: A standard that takes into account the possibility that a variety of circumstances may lead to costs that are greater than ideal.

Budgeted cost: The cost, at standard, for number of budgeted units.

Controllable overhead variance: The difference between the amount of overhead that would be included in a flexible budget for the actual level of production and the actual amount of overhead.

Ideal standard: Standards developed under the assumption that no obstacles to the production process will be encountered.

Labor efficiency variance: The difference between the standard labor hours allowed for the number of units produced and the actual number of labor hours worked times the standard labor wage rate.

Labor rate variance: The difference between the standard and actual wage rates times the actual number of labor hours worked.

Material price variance: The difference between the standard and actual prices per unit of material times the actual quantity of material used.

Material quantity variance: The difference between the standard quantity of material allowed for the number of units produced and the actual quantity of material used times the standard price of the material.

Overhead volume variance: The difference between the amount of overhead applied to production at standard and the amount of overhead included in a flexible budget for the actual level of production.

Standard cost: The cost that management believes should be incurred to produce a good or service under anticipated conditions.

Standard cost variance: The difference between standard cost and actual cost.

Variance analysis: An analysis of the difference between actual and standard cost.

Chapter 9 – True/False

_____ 1. In a standard costing system, manufactured goods are recorded at their actual product cost.

_____ 2. A primary benefit of a standard costing system is that it allows managers to compare differences between standard and actual costs.

_____ 3. The two components of the manufacturing overhead variance are the overhead volume variance and the overhead efficiency variance.

_____ 4. The two components of the direct labor variance are the labor rate variance and the labor efficiency variance.

_____ 5. If actual prices exceed standard prices, the material price variance is unfavorable.

_____ 6. If actual labor hours are less than standard hours allowed for the number of units produced, the labor efficiency variance is unfavorable.

_____ 7. The total variance for manufacturing overhead is the difference between the overhead applied to inventory at actual rates and the actual overhead incurred.

_____ 8. The controllable overhead variance is "controllable" because managers are expected to be able to control costs so that they are not substantially different from the amount that would be included in the static budget.

_____ 9. The overhead volume variance signals that the quantity of production is greater or less than anticipated when the standard overhead rate was developed.

_____ 10. A "management by exception" approach investigates only those variances that are deemed to be unfavorable.

_____ 11. A favorable variance should never be investigated.

_____ 12. At the end of the accounting period, the temporary variances should be closed directly to Retained Earnings.

Chapter 9 – Key Terms Matching

Match the terms, found in Chapter 7, with the following definitions:

a. attainable standard
b. budgeted cost
c. controllable overhead variance
d. ideal standard
e. labor efficiency variance
f. labor rate variance

g. material price variance
h. material quantity variance
i. overhead volume variance
j. standard cost
k. standard cost variance
l. variance analysis

_____ 1. The difference between the standard labor hours allowed for the number of units produced and the actual number of labor hours worked times the standard labor wage rate.

_____ 2. The difference between the amount of overhead that would be included in a flexible budget for the actual level of production and the actual amount of overhead.

_____ 3. The difference between the standard and actual wage rates times the actual number of labor hours worked.

_____ 4. The difference between the amount of overhead applied to production at standard and the amount of overhead included in a flexible budget for the actual level of production.

_____ 5. The difference between the standard and actual prices per unit of material times the actual quantity of material used.

_____ 6. The cost, at standard, for number of budgeted units.

_____ 7. An analysis of the difference between actual and standard cost.

_____ 8. Standards developed under the assumption that no obstacles to the production process will be encountered.

_____ 9. A standard that takes into account the possibility that a variety of circumstances may lead to costs that are greater than ideal.

_____ 10. The difference between the standard quantity of material allowed for the number of units produced and the actual quantity of material used times the standard price of the material.

_____ 11. The difference between standard cost and actual cost.

_____ 12. The cost that management believes should be incurred to produce a good or service under anticipated conditions.

Chapter 9 – Multiple Choice

1.   Standard costing systems generate variances for which of the following areas?
        a.   Direct labor
        b.   Direct material
        c.   Manufacturing overhead
        d.   All of the above

2.   Another term used for standard cost is
        a.   direct cost.
        b.   budgeted cost.
        c.   average cost.
        d.   all of the above.

3.   The two components for the direct material variance are
        a.   material price variance and material rate variance.
        b.   material quantity variance and material rate variance.
        c.   material price variance and material quantity variance.
        d.   material rate variance and material efficiency variance.

4.   The material price variance formula is equal to the difference between
        a.   actual price per unit and standard price per unit times the actual quantity.
        b.   total actual price and total standard price times the standard quantity.
        c.   actual quantity and standard quantity times the standard price.
        d.   none of the above.

5.   The labor efficiency variance formula is equal to the difference between the
        a.   actual number of hours worked and the standard labor hours allowed for the number
                of units produced times the standard labor wage rate.
        b.   actual number of hours worked and the standard labor hours allowed for the number
                of units produced times the actual labor wage rate.
        c.   actual wage rate and the standard wage rate times the actual number of labor hours
                worked.
        d.   actual wage rate and the standard wage rate times the standard number of labor hours
                allowed for the units produced.

6.   An unfavorable labor rate variance indicates that
        a.   actual wage rates were less than standard wage rates.
        b.   standard wage rates were less than actual wage rates.
        c.   total wages paid were less than flexible budgeted total wages.
        d.   none of the above.

7.   Purchasing low quality material may result in which of the following variances?
        a.   Unfavorable material price variance, unfavorable quantity variance
        b.   Unfavorable material price variance, favorable quantity variance
        c.   Favorable material price variance, favorable quantity variance
        d.   Favorable material price variance, unfavorable quantity variance

8.   Which of the following statements supports the use of ideal standards?
      a.   Ideal standards promote acceptance of defects and breakdowns.
      b.   Ideal standards allow for expected deviations from perfect conditions.
      c.   Ideal standards motivate employees to strive for the best possible control over production costs.
      d.   Ideal standards are supported by most managers.

9.   If a company works 500 hours less than planned, the resulting variance would be a(n)
      a.   favorable labor efficiency variance.
      b.   unfavorable labor efficiency variance.
      c.   favorable controllable variance.
      d.   unfavorable controllable variance.

10.   An unfavorable volume variances indicates that
      a.   overhead costs are out of control.
      b.   production volume was greater than planned.
      c.   production volume was less than planned.
      d.   actual overhead costs was greater than overhead applied.

11.   In recording manufacturing overhead in a standard costing system, which of the following is (are) true?
      a.   Actual overhead is recorded in the manufacturing overhead account.
      b.   Overhead is applied to Work in Process inventory at the standard cost.
      c.   The difference between actual overhead and overhead applied at standard is closed and overhead variances are identified.
      d.   All of the above are steps in recording manufacturing overhead in a standard costing system.

12.   In closing a favorable variance, which of the following statements is true?
      a.   A favorable variance reduces the amount of Cost of Goods Sold.
      b.   A favorable variance increases the amount of Cost of Goods Sold.
      c.   A favorable variance reduces the amount of Raw Materials Inventory.
      d.   A favorable variance increases the amount of Raw Materials Inventory.

Exercise 9 – 1 The Soup Fascist specializes in tomato bisque. The standards for tomatoes used in making a 10 ounce serving of bisque are given below:

Standard Quantity	.5 lbs.
Standard Price	$1.20 per lb.
Standard cost per serving	$ .60

During March 3,840 servings of tomato bisque soup were consumed by patrons. During the month, 2,000 pounds of tomatoes were purchased for $2,200. There were 20 pounds of tomatoes in ending inventory on March 31. Using the model below, compute the materials price variance and the materials quantity variance and indicate whether the variances are favorable or unfavorable.

Actual	**Actual Quantity**	**Standard**
Material Cost	**at Standard Price**	**Material Cost**

Material Price Variance   **Material Quantity Variance**

Exercise 9 – 2 Surf's Up makes surfboards from balsam wood. Standards for one surfboard are ● board feet of balsam at a cost of $5.50 per foot. During the most recent month of operations, Surf's ● purchased 63,000 board feet of balsam wood for $352,800 and produced 9,000 surfboards. At the end of ● month, Surf's Up had 4,000 board feet of balsam wood in inventory. Using the model below, compute ● materials price variance and the materials quantity variance and indicate whether the variances are favora ● or unfavorable.

Actual	**Actual Quantity**	**Standard**
Material Cost	**at Standard Price**	**Material Cost**

Material Price Variance   **Material Quantity Variance**

Exercise 9 – 3 Sleepy Head, Inc. makes down pillows. Each king pillow requires 3 pounds of down and takes .25 hours of direct labor. The standard cost of the down used by Sleepy Head is $5 per pound and the standard labor cost is $6 per hour. In 2004, Sleepy Head purchased 75,000 pounds of down for $371,250. Sleepy Head used 63,000 pounds of down in manufacturing 20,000 king pillows. Payroll reported a total of 5,600 direct labor hours at a cost of $30,800.

1.   Using the model below, compute the materials price and quantity variances and indicate whether the variances are favorable or unfavorable.

Actual **Material Cost**	**Actual Quantity** **at Standard Price**	**Standard** **Material Cost**

Material Price Variance   **Material Quantity Variance**

2.   Using the model below, compute the labor rate and efficiency variances and indicate whether the variances are favorable or unfavorable.

Actual **Labor Cost**	**Actual Quantity** **at Standard Price**	**Standard** **Labor Cost**

Labor Rate Variance   **Labor Efficiency Variance**

Problem 9 – 4 The Adobe Brick Company makes fired clay bricks to use in construction. The company uses a standard costing system and standards call for 2.5 lbs. of clay at $.60 per pound for each brick. The standard cost for labor is .1 hour at $16 per hour for each brick. Standard overhead is $.80 per unit. In 2004, Adobe anticipates production to be at a level of 150,000 bricks with fixed overhead of $45,000 and variable overhead of $ .50 per brick. During 2004, Adobe manufactured 152,000 bricks. The company purchased 400,000 pounds of clay at a cost of $232,000. Production required 390,000 pounds of clay. The cost of direct labor was $242,530 for 15,350 hours. Actual overhead for the year was $122,800.

1.   Using the model below, compute the materials price and quantity variances and indicate whether the variances are favorable or unfavorable.

Actual	Actual Quantity	Standard
Material Cost	at Standard Price	Material Cost

        Material Price Variance   **Material Quantity Variance**

2.   Using the model below, compute the labor rate and efficiency variances and indicate whether the variances are favorable or unfavorable.

Actual	Actual Quantity	Standard
Labor Cost	at Standard Price	Labor Cost

        Labor Rate Variance   **Labor Efficiency Variance**

3.   Using the model below, compute the controllable overhead variance and the overhead volume variance and indicate whether the variances are favorable or unfavorable.

Actual	Flexible Budget	Overhead Applied
Overhead Cost	Overhead	Using the standard Rate

        Controllable Overhead Variance   **Overhead Volume Variance**

Problem 9 – 5 Use the data in Problem 9-4 and your solutions to the problem to complete this problem.

1.   Prepare the journal entry to record the purchase of materials.

2.   Prepare the journal entry to record materials used in production.

3.   Prepare the journal entry to record direct labor.

4.   Prepare the journal entry to record actual overhead and overhead applied.

5.   Prepare the journal entry to close out Manufacturing Overhead and record overhead variances.

6.   Prepare the journal entry to close the variances recorded in requirements 1 through 5 to cost of goods sold.

Solutions – Chapter 9 – True/False

1. F In a standard costing system, manufactured goods are recorded at the cost that should have been incurred to produce the items.
2. T
3. F The two components of the manufacturing overhead variance are the overhead volume variance and the controllable overhead variance.
4. T
5. T
6. F If actual labor hours are less than standard hours allowed for the number of units produced, the labor efficiency variance is favorable.
7. F The total variance for manufacturing overhead is the difference between the overhead applied to inventory at standard and actual overhead costs.
8. F The controllable overhead variance is "controllable" because managers are expected to be able to control costs so that they are not substantially different from the amount that would be included in the flexible budget.
9. T
10. F A "management by exception" approach investigates only those variances (favorable and unfavorable) that they deem to be exceptional.
11. F A favorable variance does not mean it should not be investigated.
12. F At the end of the accounting period, the temporary variances should be closed to Cost of Goods Sold if the variances are not significant and to Work in Process, Finished Goods, and Cost of Goods Sold if the variances are large.

Solutions – Chapter 9 – Key Terms Matching

1.	e. labor efficiency variance	7.	l variance analysis
2.	c. controllable overhead variance	8.	d. ideal standard
3.	f. labor rate variance	9.	a. attainable standard
4.	i. overhead volume variance	10.	h material quantity variance
5.	g. material price variance	11.	k. standard cost variance
6.	b. budgeted cost	12.	j. standard cost

Solutions – Chapter 9 – Multiple Choice

1.	d	7.	d
2.	b	8.	c
3.	c	9.	a
4.	a	10.	c
5.	a	11.	d
6.	b	12.	a

Solution – Exercise 9 – 1 The Soup Fascist specializes in tomato bisque. The standards for tomatoes used in making a 10 ounce serving of bisque are given below:

Standard Quantity	.5 lbs.
Standard Price	$1.20 per lb.
Standard cost per serving	$ .60

During March 3,840 servings of tomato bisque soup were consumed by patrons. During the month, 2,000 pounds of tomatoes were purchased for $2,200. There were 20 pounds of tomatoes in ending inventory on March 31. Using the model below, compute the materials price variance and the materials quantity variance and indicate whether the variances are favorable or unfavorable.

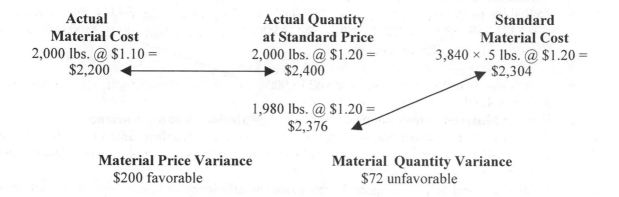

Actual Material Cost	**Actual Quantity at Standard Price**	**Standard Material Cost**
2,000 lbs. @ $1.10 = $2,200	2,000 lbs. @ $1.20 = $2,400	3,840 × .5 lbs. @ $1.20 = $2,304
	1,980 lbs. @ $1.20 = $2,376	

Material Price Variance	**Material Quantity Variance**
$200 favorable	$72 unfavorable

Solution – Exercise 9 – 2 Surf's Up makes surfboards from balsam wood. Standards for one surfboard are 6.5 board feet of balsam at a cost of $5.50 per foot. During the most recent month of operations, Surf's Up purchased 63,000 board feet of balsam wood for $352,800 and produced 9,000 surfboards. At the end of the month, Surf's Up had 4,000 board feet of balsam wood in inventory. Using the model below, compute the materials price variance and materials quantity variance and indicate whether the variances are favorable or unfavorable.

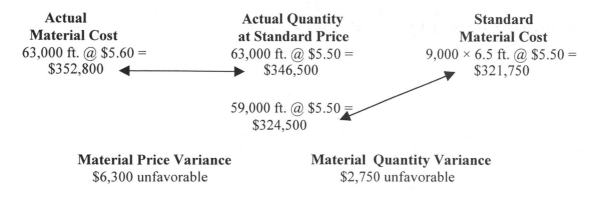

Actual Material Cost	**Actual Quantity at Standard Price**	**Standard Material Cost**
63,000 ft. @ $5.60 = $352,800	63,000 ft. @ $5.50 = $346,500	9,000 × 6.5 ft. @ $5.50 = $321,750
	59,000 ft. @ $5.50 = $324,500	

Material Price Variance	**Material Quantity Variance**
$6,300 unfavorable	$2,750 unfavorable

Solution – Exercise 9 – 3
Sleepy Head, Inc. makes down pillows. Each king pillow requires 3 pounds of down and takes .25 hours of direct labor. The standard cost of the down used by Sleepy Head is $5 per pound and the standard labor cost is $6 per hour. In 2004, Sleepy Head purchased 75,000 pounds of down for $371,250. Sleepy Head used 63,000 pounds of down in manufacturing 20,000 king pillows. Payroll reported a total of 5,600 direct labor hours at a cost of $30,800.

1.   Using the model below, compute the materials price and quantity variances and indicate whether the variances are favorable or unfavorable.

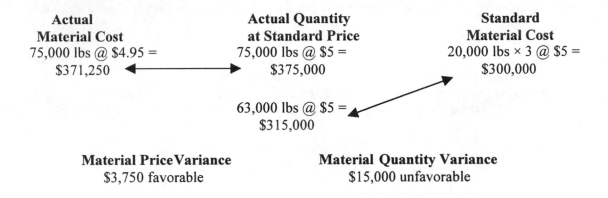

Actual Material Cost	**Actual Quantity at Standard Price**	**Standard Material Cost**
75,000 lbs @ $4.95 = $371,250	75,000 lbs @ $5 = $375,000	20,000 lbs × 3 @ $5 = $300,000
	63,000 lbs @ $5 = $315,000	

Material Price Variance	**Material Quantity Variance**
$3,750 favorable	$15,000 unfavorable

2.   Using the model below, compute the labor rate and efficiency variances and indicate whether they are favorable or unfavorable

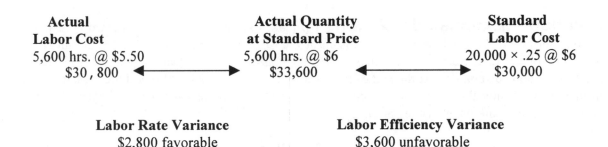

Actual Labor Cost	**Actual Quantity at Standard Price**	**Standard Labor Cost**
5,600 hrs. @ $5.50 $30,800	5,600 hrs. @ $6 $33,600	20,000 × .25 @ $6 $30,000

Labor Rate Variance	**Labor Efficiency Variance**
$2,800 favorable	$3,600 unfavorable

Solution – Problem 9 – 4

The Adobe Brick Company makes fired clay brick used in construction. The company uses a standard costing system and standards call for 2.5 lbs. of clay at $.60 per pound for each brick. The standard cost for labor is .1 hour at $16 per hour per brick. Standard overhead is $.80 per unit. In 2004, Adobe anticipates production to be at a level of 150,000 bricks with fixed overhead of $45,000 and variable overhead of $.50 per brick. During 2004, Adobe manufactured 152,000 bricks.   The company purchased 400,000 pounds of clay at a cost of $232,000. Production required 390,000 pounds of clay. The cost of direct labor was $242,530 for 15,350 hours. Actual overhead for the year was $122,800.

1.   Using the model below, compute the materials price and quantity variances and indicate whether the variances are favorable or unfavorable.

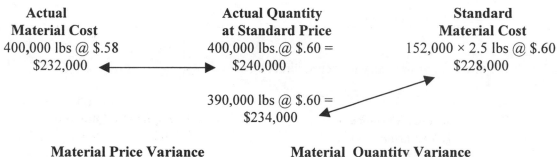

Actual Material Cost	Actual Quantity at Standard Price	Standard Material Cost
400,000 lbs @ $.58	400,000 lbs.@ $.60 =	152,000 × 2.5 lbs @ $.60
$232,000	$240,000	$228,000
	390,000 lbs @ $.60 =	
	$234,000	

Material Price Variance	**Material Quantity Variance**
$8,000 favorable	$6,000 unfavorable

2.   Using the model below, compute the labor rate and efficiency variances and indicate whether the variances are favorable or unfavorable

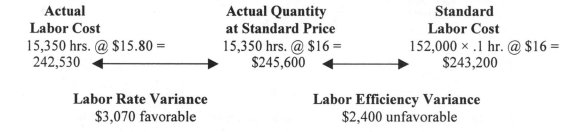

Actual Labor Cost	Actual Quantity at Standard Price	Standard Labor Cost
15,350 hrs. @ $15.80 =	15,350 hrs. @ $16 =	152,000 × .1 hr. @ $16 =
242,530	$245,600	$243,200

Labor Rate Variance	**Labor Efficiency Variance**
$3,070 favorable	$2,400 unfavorable

3.   Using the model below, compute the controllable overhead variance and the overhead volume variance and indicate whether the variances are favorable or unfavorable.

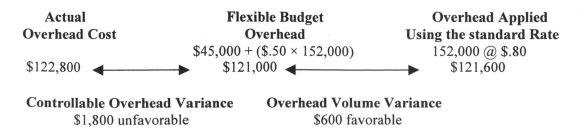

Actual Overhead Cost	Flexible Budget Overhead	Overhead Applied Using the standard Rate
	$45,000 + ($.50 × 152,000)	152,000 @ $.80
$122,800	$121,000	$121,600

Controllable Overhead Variance	**Overhead Volume Variance**
$1,800 unfavorable	$600 favorable

Solution – Problem 9 – 5

1.   Prepare the journal entry to record the purchase of materials.

Raw Material Inventory	240,000	
Materials Price Variance		8,000
Accounts Payable		232,000

2.   Prepare the journal entry to record materials used in production

Work in Process	228,000	
Materials Quantity Variance	6,000	
Raw Material Inventory		234,000

3.   Prepare the journal entry to record direct labor.

Work in Process	243,200	
Labor efficiency Variance	2,400	
Labor Rate Variance		3,070
Wages and Salaries Payable		242,530

4.   Prepare the journal entry to record actual overhead and overhead applied.

Manufacturing overhead	122,800	
Various Accounts		122,800
Work in Process	121,600	
Manufacturing Overhead		121,600

5.   Prepare the journal entry to close Manufacturing Overhead and record overhead variances

Controllable Overhead Variance	1,800	
Overhead Volume Variance		600
Manufacturing Overhead		1,200

6.   Prepare the journal entry to close the variances recorded in requirements 1 through 5 to cost of goods sold.

Materials Price Variance	8,000	
Labor Rate Variance	3,070	
Overhead Volume Variance	600	
Materials Quantity Variance		6,000
Labor Efficiency Variance		2,400
Controllable Overhead Variance		1,800
Cost of Goods Sold		1,470

CHAPTER **10**

DECENTRALIZATION AND PERFORMANCE EVALUATION

CHAPTER INTRODUCTION

Firms that grant substantial decision-making authority to the managers of subunits are referred to as **decentralized organizations**. Most firms are neither totally centralized nor totally decentralized. Decentralization is a matter of degree. To the extent that more decision-making authority is delegated to subunits, a company is more decentralized. This chapter examines various types of subunits (divisions or departments), and illustrates how performance evaluation can be used to control the behavior of subunit managers. The goal is to ensure that subunit managers make decisions that are in the best interest of the firm as a whole.

Objectives, Terms, and Discussions

LO1 *List and explain the advantages and disadvantages of decentralization.*

Advantages of decentralization include the following:
- Better information, leading to superior decisions—subunit managers often have better information than top management
- Faster response to changing circumstances—because of a subunit manager's daily involvement with customers and market conditions, he or she probably has a better understanding of how changing circumstances will affect the subunit.
- Increased motivation of managers—if managers are given broad decision-making responsibility, they may identify with their subunit and work as if they actually owned the business
- Excellent training for future top-level executives—in a decentralized organization, managers are used to making important decisions and taking responsibility for their decisions. Thus, when high-level positions in the firm become available, the firm has a ready supply of managers with the required decision-making experience.

Disadvantages of decentralization include the following:
- Costly duplication of activities—one subunit may have its own method of handling an activity, when a single, coordinated method would be more effective
- **Lack of goal congruence**—managers of subunits may pursue personal goals that are incompatible with the goals of the firm as a whole

LO2 *Explain why companies evaluate the performance of subunits and subunit managers.*

In general, companies evaluate the performance of subunits and subunit managers for two reasons. First, evaluations help identify successful operations and areas needing improvement. Managers can then continue developing successful operations and work to improve or eliminate those that do not meet expectations. Second, evaluations influence the behavior of managers. "You get what your measure" or performance measures can be used to drive the behavior of managers.

The idea of responsibility accounting, a technique that holds managers responsible only for costs and revenues that they can control, plays a prominent role in the design of accounting systems used to evaluate the performance of managers in decentralized organizations. In a decentralized organization using a responsibility accounting system, costs and revenues are traced to the organizational level where they can be controlled.

LO3 *Identify cost centers, profit centers, and investment centers.*

Subunits are sometimes referred to as **responsibility centers**, defined as organizational units responsible for the generation of revenue and/or the incurrence of costs. Responsibility centers are generally classified as being either cost centers, profit centers, or investment centers.

A **cost center** is a subunit that has responsibility for controlling costs but does not have responsibility for generating revenue. Most service departments (e.g., personnel and computer services) and production departments are classified as cost centers. A common approach to controlling cost centers is to compare their actual costs with standard or budgeted costs.

A **profit center** is a subunit that has responsibility for generating revenue as well as for controlling costs. A corporate division is an example of a profit center. Because a profit center has control over both revenue and costs, the performance of a profit center can be evaluated in terms of profitability. Evaluation in terms of profitability is useful because it motivates managers to focus their attention on ways of maximizing profitability for their subunits. Some firms evaluate profit centers using **relative performance evaluation**, which involves evaluating the profitability of each profit center relative to the profitability of other, similar profit centers. Other methods of evaluation include comparing current year income to current year target or budget amounts and comparing current year income to prior year income.

An **investment center** is a subunit that is responsible for generating revenue, controlling costs, and investing in assets. Because it is responsible for revenue, costs, and investment, an investment center is charged with earning income consistent with the amount of assets invested in the segment. Most divisions of a company can be treated as either profit centers or investment centers. If the division manager can significantly influence decisions affecting investment in divisional assets, the division should be considered an investment center. Although central management generally has final approval for major investments, investment center managers generally play a major role in determining the level of inventory, the level of accounts receivable, and the investment in capital assets held by the investment center. Thus, investment center managers are generally held responsible for earning a return on these assets.

LO4   *Calculate and interpret return on investment (ROI).*

One of the primary tools for evaluating the performance of investment centers is **return on investment (ROI).** ROI is calculated as the ratio of investment center income to invested capital. ROI has an advantage over income as a measure of performance because it focuses the attention of managers not only on income, but also on investment.

$$ROI = \frac{Income}{Invested\ Capital}$$

Some companies break ROI down into two components: profit margin and investment turnover. **Profit margin** is the ratio of income to sales, while **investment turnover** is the ratio of sales to invested capital. Managers can take actions to improve ROI in two ways:
- improve income earned on each dollar of sales (i.e., increase the margin) or
- generate more sales for each dollar invested (i.e., increase turnover).

$$ROI = \frac{Income}{Sales} \times \frac{Sales}{Invested\ capital}$$

In calculating ROI, companies measure "income" in a variety of ways. One way is to measure investment center income as net operating profit after taxes, known as **NOPAT.** Calculating NOPAT involves adding interest expense back to net income and deducting the tax savings related to the interest expense from net income. A benefit of NOPAT is that it does not hold the investment center managers responsible for interest expense since these managers frequently do not have responsibility for decisions related to financing their operations.

Although using ROI has its advantages, one problem with using ROI is that investments in assets is typically measured using historical costs. As assets become fully depreciated, the measure of investment becomes very low, and ROI becomes quite high. Some critics of ROI have suggested that undue emphasis on ROI may lead managers to delay the purchase of modern equipment needed to stay competitive.

LO5   *Explain why using a measure of profit to evaluate performance can lead to overinvestment and why using a measure of return on investment (ROI) can lead to underinvestment.*

If managers are evaluated in terms of growth in profit, they may be motivated to make investments that earn a return that is less than the cost of capital—that is, they may overinvest in assets. A solution to the overinvestment problem is to evaluate managers in terms of ROI. Managers will not be motivated to take on projects that have a low return just to increase profit if they are evaluated in terms of the return they earn. As discussed above, however, ROI has its own problems. Using ROI may lead to underinvestment—that is, managers may pass up projects that earn a return that is greater than the cost of capital. Other approaches that firms may use instead of a measure of profit or ROI involve the use of residual income, economic value added, or a Balanced Scorecard.

LO6   *Calculate and interpret residual income (RI) and economic value added (EVA).*

Residual income, or RI, is the net operating profit after taxes of an investment center in excess of the profit required for the level of investment (NOPAT minus required profit). To calculate residual income, a required rate of return—the rate of return that a company believes should be earned on its investment—must be specified; this is generally the cost of capital for the investment center. A number of measures of investment can be used. The formula for calculating RI is:

$$\text{Residual income} = \text{NOPAT} - \text{Required profit}$$

$$\text{Where Required profit} = \text{cost of capital} \times \text{investment}$$

Economic value added, also called EVA, is a performance measure developed by the consulting firm, Stern Stewart. EVA is simply residual income adjusted for "accounting distortions." An example of an accounting distortion is the treatment of research and development (R&D). For financial purposes, R&D is expensed when incurred. With EVA, R&D is capitalized as an asset and expensed through amortization over future periods.

LO7 *Explain the potential benefits of using a Balanced Scorecard to assess performance.*

A problem with assessing performance with financial measures like profit, ROI, RI, and EVA is that financial measures focus on past financial performance rather than on what managers are doing to create future shareholder value. Essentially, a **Balanced Scorecard** is a set of performance measures constructed for four dimensions of performance. The dimensions are financial, customer, internal process, and innovation. A company will typically develop three to five performance measures for each dimension, and the measures are tied to the company's strategy for success.

LOA1 *Discuss the use of market price, variable cost, full cost plus profit, and negotiation in setting transfer prices.*

The price that is used to value internal transfers of goods or services is referred to as a **transfer price**. A number of different approaches are taken to setting transfer prices. The primary alternatives are based on market prices, variable costs, full cost plus profit, and negotiated prices. Which of the transfer prices is most appropriate depends on the circumstances.

The market price of an item can be used as the transfer price. The external market price is an excellent internal transfer price because it allows both the buying division and the selling division to be treated as "stand-alone," independent companies. Market prices are perceived as fair and reasonable by both the buying and the selling divisions. In addition, market price is a good transfer price because it equals the opportunity cost.

If the transferred product is unique and is not sold by the producing division in the open market, no market price exists. The variable cost of producing the transferred good may be the best transfer price in this situation. Selecting the variable cost of production as the transfer price is appropriate because it conveys accurate opportunity cost information.

A problem with using variable cost as the transfer price is that the selling division cannot earn a profit on production of the transferred product. Thus, many companies add a profit margin to the full cost of an item and use the resulting amount as the transfer price.

To encourage the sense of autonomy, some companies allow division managers to negotiate a transfer price. A disadvantage of this method is that the resulting transfer price may reflect the relative negotiating skills of the subunit managers and fail to reflect the underlying opportunity cost associated with producing a good and transferring it internally.

Review of Key Terms

Balanced scorecard: A set of performance measures (linked to a company's strategy) for four categories: financial, customer, internal processes, and innovation.

Cost center: A business segment responsible for controlling costs, not for generating revenues.

Decentralized organization: A firm that grants substantial decision-making authority to the managers of subunits.

Economic value added (EVA): A performance measure equal to net operating profit after taxes (adjusted for accounting distortions) less a charge based on the level of investment.

Investment center: A business segment responsible for generating revenue, controlling costs, and investing in assets.

Investment turnover: A performance measure equal to sales divided by invested capital.

Lack of goal congruence: A situation where managers pursue personal goals that are incompatible with the goals of the company as a whole.

NOPAT: Net operating profit after taxes.

Profit center: A business segment responsible for generating revenue as well as for controlling cost.

Profit margin: Net income divided by revenue.

Relative performance evaluation: The evaluation of a subunit in comparison to similar subunits within a company.

Residual income (RI): A performance measure equal to NOPAT less a charge for the level of investment.

Responsibility center: Organizational units responsible for the generation of revenue or for the incurrence of costs.

Return on investment (ROI): A performance measure equal to investment center income divided by invested capital

Transfer price: The price used to value internal transfers of goods or services.

Chapter 10 – True/False

_T_ 1. An advantage of decentralization is that it provides excellent training for future top-level executives.

_F_ 2. The idea of responsibility accounting is not appropriate in a decentralized organization.

_F_ 3. Responsibility centers are generally classified as being cost centers, revenue centers, or profit centers.

_F_ 4. Most service departments are classified as investment centers.

_T_ 5. If the division manager can significantly influence decisions affecting investments in division assets, the division should be considered an investment center.

_T_ 6. ROI has an advantage over income as a measure of performance because it focuses the attention of managers investment instead of income.

_T_ 7. A benefit of NOPAT is that it does not hold investment center managers responsible for interest expense since these managers frequently do not have responsibility for decisions related to financing their operations.

_F_ 8. An advantage of using ROI is that investment in assets is typically measured using historical costs.

_T_ 9. If managers are evaluated in terms of growth in profit, they may be motivated to overinvest on assets.

_T_ 10. EVA is simply net income adjusted for "tax distortions."

_T_ 11. Market price is a good transfer price because it equals the opportunity cost.

_T_ 12. A problem with using variable cost as a transfer price is that the selling division cannot earn a profit on production of a transferred product.

Chapter 10 – Key Terms Matching

Match the terms found in Chapter 10 with the following definitions:

a. balanced scorecard
b. cost center
c. decentralized organization
d. economic value added (EVA)
e. investment center
f. investment turnover

g. NOPAT
h. profit center
i. relative performance evaluation
j. residual income
k. responsibility center
l. transfer price

_H_ 1. A business segment responsible for generating revenue as well as for controlling costs.

_C_ 2. A firm that grants substantial decision-making authority to the managers of subunits.

_F_ 3. A performance measure equal to sales divided by invested capital.

_L_ 4. The price used to value internal transfers of goods or services.

_B_ 5. A business segment responsible for controlling costs, not for generating revenues.

_J_ 6. A performance measure equal to NOPAT less a charge for the level of investment.

_A_ 7. A set of performance measures for four categories: financial, customer, internal processes, and innovation.

_G_ 8. Net operating profit after taxes.

_D_ 9. A performance measure equal to net operating profit after taxes (adjusted for accounting distortions) less a charge based on the level of investment.

_K_ 10. Organizational units responsible for the generation of revenue or for the incurrence of costs.

_E_ 11. A business segment responsible for generating revenue, controlling costs, and investing in assets.

_I_ 12. The evaluation of a subunit in comparison to similar subunits within a company.

Chapter 10 – Multiple Choice

1.   Which of the following is not an advantage of decentralization?
      a.   Better information leading to superior decisions
      b.   Faster response to changing circumstances
      c.   Increased motivation of managers
      d.   Elimination of duplication of activities

2.   Which of the following is a disadvantage of decentralization?
      a.   Lack of goal congruence
      b.   Failure to provide training for future top-level executives
      c.   Costly duplication of activities
      d.   Both a and c

3.   Which of the following is not a reason companies evaluate the performance of subunits and subunit managers?
      a.   Evaluations help identify successful operations
      b.   Evaluations help identify areas needing improvement
      c.   Evaluations provide a means for punishment for poor managers
      d.   Evaluations influence the behavior of managers

4.   Subunits are often referred to as
      a.   opportunity units.
      b.   responsibility centers.
      c.   control centers.
      d.   performance units.

5.   Which of the following is not a classification of a responsibility center?
      a.   Cost center
      b.   Profit center
      c.   Control center
      d.   Investment center

6.   Which of the following is an example of a profit center?
      a.   A corporate division
      b.   A personnel department   *cost center*
      c.   A computer center
      d.   Both a and c

7.   The formula for calculating ROI is
      a.   income divided by sales.
      b.   income divided by invested capital.
      c.   sales divided by income.
      d.   sales divided by invested capital.

8.   Profit margin is the ratio of
      a.   income to sales.
      b.   sales to invested capital.
      c.   cost of goods sold to sales.
      d.   income to invested capital.

9.   In calculating economic value added, an example of an accounting distortion is
   a.   depreciation.
   b.   accrued liabilities.
   c.   research and development expenses.
   d.   all of the above.

10.   Which of the following is not an advantage of using market price as the transfer price?
   a.   It allows the buying division and the selling division to be treated as independent companies.
   b.   Market prices are perceived as fair and reasonable by both the buying and selling divisions.
   c.   Market price equals the opportunity cost.
   d.   All of the above are advantages of using market price as the transfer price.

11.   Which of the following is a disadvantage of using a negotiated price as the transfer price?
   a.   Negotiated prices are perceived as fair and reasonable by both the buying and selling divisions.
   b.   Negotiated prices always equal the opportunity cost.
   c.   Negotiated prices may reflect the negotiating skills of the subunit managers and fail to reflect the underlying opportunity cost associated with producing a good and transferring it internally.
   d.   None of the above are disadvantages of using a negotiated price as the transfer price.

12.   A justification for measuring invested capital as total assets less noninterest-bearing current liabilities is
   a.   noninterest-bearing liabilities do not have a tax effect on net income.
   b.   interest-bearing liabilities reduce the cost of the investment in assets.
   c.   noninterest-bearing liabilities are considered a "free" source of funds and reduce the cost of the investment in assets.
   d.   noninterest-bearing liabilities do not affect cash.

Exercise 10 – 1 Surf's Up is a division of Oceania. During 2004, Surf's Up had a net income of $720,000. Interest expense of $50,000 was included in the computation of net income. The company's tax rate is 20%. Total assets of the surfboard division are $7,000,000, current liabilities are $1,600,000 and $1,000,000 of the current liabilities are noninterest-bearing.

1.   Calculate NOPAT for Surf's Up.

2.   Calculate invested capital for Surf's Up.

3.   Calculate ROI for Surf's Up.

Exercise 10 – 2 For the year 2004, Richard's Backpacks had income as follows:

Sales	$800,000
Less:	
Cost of goods sold	480,000
Selling and administrative expense	10,000
Interest expense	2,000
Income before taxes	308,000
Less income taxes	61,600
Net income	$246,400

Total assets were $1,604,000 and noninterest-bearing current liabilities were $4,000. The company has a required rate of return on capital equal to 12%.

1.   Calculate NOPAT for Richard's Backpacks.

2.   Calculate invested capital for Richard's Backpacks.

3.   Calculate ROI for Richard's Backpacks.

Thinking Exercise 10 – 3 Casual observation suggests that there are businesses which maximize profit margin while others maximize turnover. Look through your local phone book and find three businesses that you think strive to maximize profit margin and find three that strive to maximize turnover.

Problem 10 – 4   The Hunter Motor Corporation produces two automobiles–Basic and Deluxe. The following information relates to the operations for Hunter Motors for the year 2004.

Total assets	$2,928,570	$1,830,000
Noninterest-bearing current liabilities	14,285	15,000
Net income	808,000	505,000
Interest expense	10,000	4,000
Sales	10,200,000	3,630,000
Tax rate	20%	20%

1.   Compute the profit margin for both Basic and Deluxe.

2.   Compute the turnover for both Basic and Deluxe.

3.   Compute the ROI for both Basic and Deluxe.

Problem 10 – 5   The Soup Fascist has two locations, one in Midtown and one Uptown. Data on the two restaurants are given below:

	Midtown	Uptown
Sales	$6,750,000	$15,000,000
NOPAT	438,750	1,350,000
Invested Capital	2,250,000	7,500,000
Rate of Return	16%	16%

1.   Compute the ROI for each location.

2.   Compute the residual income for each location.

3.   Is Uptown's greater residual income an indication that it is managed better?

Solutions – True/False

1. T
2. F   The idea of responsibility accounting plays a prominent role in the design of accounting systems used to evaluate the performance of managers in a decentralized organization.
3. F   Responsibility centers are generally classified as being cost center, profit centers, or investment centers.
4. F   Most service departments are classified as cost centers.
5. T
6. F   ROI has an advantage over income as a measure of performance because it focuses the attention of managers not only on income, but also on investment.
7. T
8. F   A problem with using ROI is that investment in assets is typically measured using historical costs.
9. T
10. F   EVA is simply residual income adjusted for "accounting distortions."
11. T
12. T

Solutions – Key Terms Matching

1.	h. profit center	7.	a. balanced scorecard
2.	c. decentralized organization	8.	g. NOPAT
3.	f. investment turnover	9.	d. economic value added (EVA)
4.	l. transfer price	10.	k. responsibility center
5.	b. cost center	11.	e. investment center
6.	j. residual income	12.	i. relative performance evaluation

Solutions – Chapter 10 – Multiple Choice

1.	d	7.	b
2.	d	8.	a
3.	c	9.	c
4.	b	10.	d
5.	c	11.	c
6.	a	12.	c

Solution – Exercise 10 – 1
Surf's Up is a division of Oceania. During 2004, Surf's Up had a net income of $720,000. Interest expense of $50,000 was included in the computation of net income. The company's tax rate is 20%. Total assets of the surf board division are $7,000,000, current liabilities are $1,600,000 and $1,000,000 of the current liabilities are noninterest-bearing.

1.   Calculate NOPAT for Surf's Up.

Net Income	$ 720,000
+ Interest expense	50,000
- Tax savings related interest	10,000
NOPAT	$ 760,000

2.   Calculate invested capital for Surf's Up.

Total assets	$7,000,000
- Noninterest-bearing current liabilities	1,000,000
Invested capital	$6,000,000

3.   Calculate ROI for Surf's Up.

$$\frac{\text{Income} \quad \$\ 720,000}{\text{Invested Capital} \quad \$6,000,000} = 12\%$$

Solution – Exercise 10 – 2 For the year 2004, Richard's Backpacks had income as follows:

Sales	$800,000
Less:	
Cost of goods sold	480,000
Selling and administrative expense	10,000
Interest expense	2,000
Income before taxes	308,000
Less income taxes	61,600
Net income	$246,400

Total assets were $1,604,000 and noninterest-bearing current liabilities were $4,000. The company has a required rate of return on capital equal to 12%.

1.   Calculate NOPAT for Richard's Backpacks.

Net Income	$ 246,400
+ Interest expense	2,000
- Tax savings related interest	400
NOPAT	$ 248,000

2.   Calculate invested capital for Richard's Backpacks.

Total assets	$1,604,000
- Noninterest-bearing current liabilities	4,000
Invested capital	$1,600,000

3.   Calculate ROI for Richard's Backpacks.

$$\frac{NOPAT\ \$248,000}{Sales\ \ \$800,000} \times \frac{Sales\ \ \$\ 800,000}{Invested\ Capital\ \$1,600,000} = \frac{NOPAT\ \ \$\ 248,000}{Invested\ Capital\ \$1,600,000}$$

$$31\% \times 50\% = 15.5\%$$

Solution – Thinking Exercise 10 – 3   Casual observation suggests that there are businesses that maximize profit margin while others maximize turnover. Look through your local phone book and find three businesses that you think strive to maximize profit margin and find three that strive to maximize turnover.

Profit Margin	Turnover
Luxury automobile dealers	Discount department stores
Boat dealers	Discount building supply stores
Mobile home dealers	Fast food restaurants
Jewelers	Discount optical stores
Furriers	Discount pharmacies

Solution – Problem 10 – 4

The Hunter Motor Corporation produces two automobiles–Basic and Deluxe. The following information relates to the operations for Hunter Motors for the year 2004.

Total assets	$2,928,570	$1,830,000
Noninterest-bearing current liabilities	14,285	15,000
Net income	808,000	505,000
Interest expense	10,000	4,000
Sales	10,200,000	3,630,000
Tax rate	20%	20%

1.   Compute the profit margin for both Basic and Deluxe.

Basic

$$\frac{\$\ 816,000}{\$10,200,000} = 8\%$$

Deluxe

$$\frac{\$\ 508,200}{\$3,630,000} = 14\%$$

2.   Compute the turnover for both Basic and Deluxe.

Basic

$$\frac{\$10,200,000}{\$\ 2,914,285} = 3.5$$

Deluxe

$$\frac{\$3,630,000}{\$1,815,000} = 2$$

3.   Compute the ROI for both Basic and Deluxe.

Basic

$$\frac{\$\ 816,000}{\$10,200,000} \times \frac{\$10,200,000}{\$\ 2,914,285} = 28\%$$

Deluxe

$$\frac{\$\ 508,200}{\$3,630,000} \times \frac{\$3,630,000}{\$1,815,000} = 28\%$$

Solution – Problem 10 – 5 The Soup Fascist has two locations, one in Midtown and one Uptown. Data on the two restaurants are given below:

	Midtown	Uptown
Sales	$6,750,000	$15,000,000
NOPAT	438,750	1,350,000
Invested Capital	2,250,000	7,500,000
Rate of Return	16%	16%

1. Compute the ROI for each location.

Midtown

$$\frac{\$\ 438,750}{\$6,750,000} \times \frac{\$6,750,000}{\$2,250,000} = 19.5\%$$

Uptown

$$\frac{\$\ 1,350,000}{\$15,000,000} \times \frac{\$15,000,000}{\$\ 7,500,000} = 18\%$$

2. Compute the residual income for each location.

$$\$2,250,000 \times .16 = \frac{\begin{array}{r}\$438,750 \\ 360,000\end{array}}{\$\ 78,750}$$

$$\$7,500,000 \times .16 = \frac{\begin{array}{r}\$1,350,000 \\ 1,200,000\end{array}}{\$\ 150,000}$$

3. Is Uptown's greater residual income an indication that it is managed better?

No. Because the Uptown restaurant is larger than the Midtown restaurant one would expect it to have a greater amount of residual income.

Notes

Notes

Notes

Notes

Notes

Notes